Author's contact details:

hello@kindnessmatters.co.uk

www.kindnessmatters.co.uk

Edited by Jo Watson

www.agoodwriteup.com

Cover Design and Artwork by

Arthur Luke www.arthurluke.co.uk

Proofreader Umbreen Ali

KINDNESS MATTERS

John Magee

ENDORSEMENTS

"John Magee's work is truly inspirational. If more people thought like John, the world would be a much better place."
Nathan Chan - CEO & founder of Foundr Magazine

More than a 'feel good' guide, Kindness Matters offers a whole new way to see yourself and the world. It can bring more than a smile to your life. Motivational and uplifting, this book is a must read.
Maureen Bateson - Executive member Children's services

"Want to learn how to feel better in yourself and in the workplace? Then you need to read this book. Not only is John a true friend; he is a collaborator, a fellow speaker with his witty Irish charm. His book, 'Kindness Matters', can and will motivate any individual or team to understand the many positive benefits from practicing daily acts of kindness in the workplace and in life"
Steve Gray CEO - Training 2000

"If you could do just one thing to enrich your own life and those around you, it would be to take the advice of this book to live kindly. The kindness we give to others marks a powerful contribution we can make to the heart of the world at large. I wholeheartedly recommend this book."
Beck Ray Founder of Happi Habits. www.happihabits.com.

KINDNESSMATTERS

ENDORSEMENTS

Thank You, John, for writing such an Inspirational book. I plan on recommending your 30 day challenge to friends, families and work colleagues because I personally believe it will have an impact on them like it has on me and many others.

Paul Jackson - Author Ho'oponopono Secrets

You owe it to yourself to take the 30 day challenge. From the moment you open this treasure chest, the magic will manifest into your life. Full of gems and tools to keep you connected to yourself whilst looking after your family.

Amanda Meachin - CEO Community and Business Partners

Our days are happier when we give people a bit of our heart rather than a piece of our mind. The 30 Day Challenge is addictive. There isn't a better feeling than being the reason someone had a great day. We rise by lifting others

Adam Catterall - Multi Award winning broadcaster and Founder of Fight Disciples

What I love about the 30 Day Challenge is how it highlights the fact that whatever your job is, you can always make a conscious effort to sprinkle what John describes as "covert acts of kindness" into your daily work and life - pure genius!

Mike Kawula CEO & Founder Social Quant

KINDNESSMATTERS

**I would like to dedicate this book to my beautiful sister,
Kathleen Sarah Magee.**

1974 – 2014 RIP

381 KSM

My beautiful Kathleen; one of the kindest and most generous
human beings I knew, and who I miss more than
words can ever say.

KINDNESSMATTERS

PREFACE

'One person can change the world' - John Magee

"John Magee?! Ha! He's just another loose cannon on a project."

To the person I overheard say this about me to a group of my peers, I cannot thank you enough for your words.

To hear such words at all can sting, but to hear them tumble out of the mouth of someone who you formerly trusted as they use those words to sow seeds of doubt against you is a true example of hurt. It's sad to think that most of us have been there.

However, once I'd dealt with the initial shock of this 'behind my back' chatter, I chose to take these words into my heart and mind in the most positive way I could think of - and I used them as a key ingredient in the recipe that has given me the strength to put this book together for you today.

As the writer and humorist, Zero Dean, famously said:
"Not everyone will understand your journey. That's fine. It's not their journey to make sense of. It's yours."

With this quote in mind, I don't hold any ill feeling towards my critic. I have since sent her a copy of this book to show her that, if anything, her words spurred me on to prove that this 'loose cannon' could go on to change the world.
Kill them with kindness, John.

KINDNESSMATTERS

THE KINDNESS MATTERS MISSION

Transform one million lives, one day at a time

In addition to donating a percentage of the royalties from each copy of Kindness Matters to the CoppaFeel! Breast Cancer Charity (www.coppafeel.org), thousands of copies of the Kindness Matters book have been donated to community-based projects whom it is thought will benefit from inspiration and transformation. Our mission is to get Kindness Matters into the hands of one million people, so that we can literally change one million lives; one act of kindness at a time.

Thank you so much for your kind support.

KINDNESSMATTERS

CONTENTS

KINDNESSMATTERS

"Just imagine when you look back on your life
and recollect on all the good you did.
How good you will feel."

- John Magee

INTRODUCTION

Have you ever worked so hard at something and given it your all only to find that you don't appear to be making any progress?

Have you ever believed so strongly in something that you knew in your gut was absolutely the right thing to do, but you couldn't find anyone or anything to back you up?

Do you ever have those days, months or even years when you just ask yourself if what you are doing is even making any difference at all?

I believe we all have these questions, brick walls and testing moments in life. However I also believe that deep down we all have the ability to rise above all of these things in order to become role models and to leave a legacy behind for our children as well as future generations.

I am not saying I have all the answers or techniques for overcoming every challenge, but what I would like for you to always keep in mind is this:

Kindness Matters. It is in giving kindness that you will receive.

Keep going, friends, and let me help you. Let me guide you on the right path by introducing you to this very book; a book I know you will enjoy and gain much from.

INTRODUCTION

The aim of this book is to encourage you to make a commitment and conscious effort to carry out acts of kindness and to engage with the principle of the 'Kindness Matters 30 Day challenge'.

A lot of people say to me "I always perform acts of kindness" and this is good to hear.

What I hope, is that this book will make you more consciously aware to look for daily opportunities to – as we say in our Facebook community – "Ramp up your RAOK *(Random acts of kindness)*". Also, when they are done to you, don't forget to pay that RAOK forward!

It is important I mention that once you have completed your Thirty Days, you do not have to stop your good-will! The aim of the Thirty Days vision is to help you create a new synaptic habit of consciously performing more acts of kindness – both random and planned – throughout your daily life.

In the book, you will find lots of heart-warming stories of real life RAOK, as well as daily hints, tips and original ways to apply more acts of kindness and RAOK to your daily routine. However, like any exercise, this will take time and commitment.

For me, there is no better feeling than knowing that when you have gone out of your way to help another person, with no expectation of reward, how good it feels to know you have that

KINDNESSMATTERS

power to take control of your actions and to apply them in a manner which reaps positive consequences as a result.

My invitation to you is to challenge yourself, your family, your friends and every human being you come into contact with, to embrace and share the global vision of the 'Kindness Matters 30 Day challenge'. It is crucial for you to go out of your way each day and take action to apply a minimum of one daily act of kindness – random or planned - with absolutely no expectation of reward.

What's the worst that could happen?

"Carry out random acts of kindness, with no expectation of reward, safe in the knowledge that one day someone might do the same for you." - Princess Diana

"Kindness is the gift that keeps on giving."

- John Magee

Timeline

TIMELINE

So, you've read the introduction to this book. Now let me take you back in time so that you can truly see where my vision for the philosophy that 'Kindness Matters' was born.

In 2001, my path crossed with a gentleman by the name of David Dunn. At that point, David was the top goal scorer and massive fan favourite at my local English Premier League football club, Blackburn Rovers FC. What made David even more of a legend was that he had been born and bred right here in the town he played for - something not many top level players can say about the club they represent. When I think back, an act of kindness that David would go on to show me during our first ever contact would be a massive turning point in my life later on.

Around the time I met David, I was working on the news desk of my local newspaper, The Lancashire Evening Telegraph. I was engaged to be married, I had my first child, Millie, and my second child, Lucas, was on his way! I loved my job and the people I worked with. Life was good.

As we know, these periods of settlement and happiness can change within the timeframe of a phone call, and, I remember the day I took such a call from my friend Shaun. Shaun was sobbing, and as he broke down, he poured his heart out to me regarding some tragic news involving his sister, Michelle. Michelle had been diagnosed with terminal breast cancer.

Upon hearing and attempting to process the news, I felt physically sick. Shaun was one of my closest friends, and Michelle was like a sister to me.

Terminal. When you hear that word, there's no positive spin you can put on it. Whatever did or didn't happen next, we were going to lose Michelle and the world was going to lose a truly kind spirit.

As well as an amazing sister, Michelle was a truly kind and compassionate mother who had raised two beautiful young daughters who I thought the world of. Through my own tears, I vowed to Shaun that I would do everything I could to help him through this awful time.

That night, I couldn't stop thinking about Michelle's poor kids and what would happen to them after her imminent death. I thought back to when, in a more energetic life, I had gone through with a charity parachute jump to raise money for an appeal looking after premature babies and their families.

That event had made me feel so good, and I was desperate to feel good again right now by doing something equally full of impact and kindness.

The cogs started turning and I raced to my office at the Telegraph to see if I could use my links and contacts to promote a fundraiser that I would carry out in aid of Shaun, Michelle and the kids.

I began to contact everyone I knew. A colleague at the news desk told me she was on first name terms with local footballing legend, David Dunn. I wasn't hopeful he would help me, as footballers are positively inundated with requests from random strangers on a daily basis, asking for support, money, publicity, donations, appearances etc. I had nothing to lose, and, on the off-chance that David was able to help me, it would mean some high profile publicity for our cause.

I got David's phone number and, when he answered after two rings, I launched into a garbled tale about the wonderful Michelle and my plight to do the right thing by her. I was astounded that David cut me short and told me he'd be honoured to help in any way he could, informing me that he had not long lost his Aunty to terminal breast Cancer - the same disease that Michelle had.

Stunned but delighted, I thanked David profusely and vowed to call him back with a plan. Ultimately, we settled on running a three-day fundraiser at my friend Ming's Chinese restaurant, Mister Fu's, as we both loved the place and knew it would cater for the largest possible numbers. Over those three days, we raised over £5000 for Breakthrough Breast Cancer and for Michelle's family. Although any amount of money would have been lovely, I cannot help thinking that this was always going

KINDNESSMATTERS

to be grander with someone like David using his influence and kindness. To my mind, his generosity of spirit made a huge impact.

David and I became good friends, and with my ideas and his generosity and influence, we became a self-proclaimed team of dreams to do kind things in the community we had both grown up in. For someone with so much celebrity status in our town, David had never lost a jot of who he was or where he had come from.

We always knew the day would come, but it wasn't long before Michelle lost her battle with Cancer. She was 37. The world had, in my eyes, lost a true kindness ambassador. I wanted to go out and make it my mission to make sure that I could do something - anything - to fill that void and that is why, to this day, I will work to inspire others to be just a little bit more like Michelle.

"It is said that the darkest hour of the night comes just before dawn" - Thomas Fuller

Have you ever had one of those days in your life where life is rocking, and then one of those days where it all turns to rubbish? Or, have you ever had one of those years?

2005

I was living the life of my dreams. I was married with three beautiful children, I had just recently bought a lovely little house in an amazing area, and then to put the icing on the cake I landed a once in a lifetime dream job at the largest plastic plumbing manufacturers in the world. It was such a good feeling, phoning my wife on the way home from the interview. When I gave her the news, we were both screaming and shouting in absolute joy, saying what we were going to do for our future and how this would help the kids with their education.

Within no time at all, I became the top-selling regional sales manager for the company and began to smash all my targets out of the water. The company boss, Mark Wright, was astounded by my resilience and strong desire to succeed. I even broke the all-time company record for product sales.

Mark and I were very similar in character and wanted to be the best version of ourselves that we could be. Unfortunately, this did not go down well with some of my team and my direct manager took it quite personally that I was so enthusiastic and wanted to rise through the ranks. I remember meeting him for a coffee and him saying, "Listen John, it's good to have someone like yourself on the team with so much energy, but I need you to 'play the game'. I wasn't sure what he meant, and so he bluntly told me that I was making everyone else look bad. I left our

KINDNESSMATTERS

meeting a little confused, as I was just being myself, but it was quite clear that my positive mindset and enthusiasm wasn't as well received by my colleagues as it was with my clients.

It looked like I'd have to 'play the game' after all.

2006

I got a phone call out of the blue from my previous Managing Director, Tim Smith. Tim had just sold his plumbing company for 30 million pounds, and was looking at setting up a new venture. He had called me to see if David Dunn and I wanted to be in on his proposal. It was intriguing, but I told Tim I pretty much had a job for life where I was, and that in having a new family, getting involved in anything at ground level was just too risky. Tim understood and instead we arranged to have a friendly catch-up over a coffee when he was next up north.

True to his word, Tim came up north and we met for coffee. Within minutes of chit-chat, he had given me a copy of his business plan, and encouraged me to think about it again - this time sharing it with my wife Donna. Tim wanted to set up two high-end bathroom companies. He wanted to combine his 30 years' experience with Dunny's celebrity status and my sales reputation. He was then looking to float each company for 5 million in the next five years. I was hooked in. I remember getting home and telling Donna we were going to be millionaires. I talked incessantly about paying off the mortgage and putting the kids through top private education. I spun tales of family holidays and nice cars, and university life for each of our beautiful kids. Donna responded coolly and calmly, and reminded me that too much hard work had already gone into getting us where we were at that point, and that a change would be too risky anyway owing to credit card bills and nursery fees etc. I pleaded with her, but she wouldn't budge.

That night, I called my dad for advice - something I had never done before. He told me to take the opportunity because I would only get one life and it shouldn't hold any regrets.

Between Donna and my dad, I sided with my dad. I phoned my boss, thanked him for everything but said I'd be leaving. Within days, Tim, Dunny and I had found a fantastic location to base the new bathroom business from in the Lake District, some hundred or so miles away from home. It took no time at all to get the business up and running, and for a good while it seemed like we were making money for fun. Life couldn't get any better.

2007

An intense year. My team were creating amazing bathrooms, the reputation was outstanding and I was working with some great mates along the way. I have to admit though, that the long

KINDNESSMATTERS

commute to the Lake District each day, and minimal amounts of time with my wife and kids were all beginning to take their toll. My wife was getting frustrated with it all and we argued almost daily. To counteract the feelings, I had started drinking excessive amounts of alcohol.

Friends began telling me how unhappy Donna had become and hinted at the fact that she'd never wanted me to start the business in the first place and was now scared our marriage was failing. I had mixed emotions about this, because I had set up the business purely to make sure my family would be okay and to give us all a decent future.

One day, I came home late from work. The kids were in the bath and Donna and I almost instantly ended up in a full on blazing argument. I accused her of seeing somebody else. I don't know why. One thing led to another, as we stormed through the house up to the bathroom, carrying the argument on as we went to tend to the kids. I'm ashamed to admit that I then lunged at Donna in anger. The kids saw everything. I was so ashamed of the act and the audience; I just broke down, telling Donna we couldn't do this anymore.

I stormed out of the house feeling lost, upset and a failure. How could I do this to my own wife and kids after all I had experienced as a child in a family of drunken domestic violence? I vowed to myself that I would not turn out like Dad, and instead made a decision to file for divorce.

2008

The year owned one of the worst weeks of my life. I remember my cousin Lee phoning to ask about the business. I kept it positive, but in truth, our business boom had not lasted long and we were only roughly breaking even. Although I held this back from Lee, he took the opportunity to tell me that there was a global recession coming and that I'd probably need to restructure my team of 14 staff. I had some thinking to do.

Within a few days, the Bank phoned and told me they needed to pull my 30k overdraft. Again, this was linked to the impending global recession. I became stressed and tried to bargain with him, telling him I had staff to pay and a family to support, but of course there was nothing he could do - it was business, nothing personal.

I started to witness my world implode. My marriage had failed; my business was failing and so it looked like I was truly losing everything I held dear and had worked for. I drove home that night to face the music with my soon to be ex-wife and the kids, and explained to my children that Daddy was moving out of the house. My son, Lucas, was only four and thought the prospect of having two houses to live in was "cool". My daughter, Millie, on the other hand, was a little older and wiser, and was not happy at all. She sobbed so hard that the tears appeared to crack her face.

Walking out of that house the next day, I faced the very real prospect of losing my family, my livelihood and even a place to call home.

2009 - 2012

My Cousin Lee owned a letting agency called E-den Lettings. He helped me get myself settled in a bedsit. It wasn't much but it was better than nothing. I phoned my old boss to see if there was any chance of getting my old job back, but of course that door was now closed.

I did manage to get a stroke of luck, though. I met one of my old friends, Dwayne Hill, who was a boss at a global photocopying firm. He had known me a long time and told me he could employ me. Although I didn't fancy selling photocopiers for a career, I wasn't in a position to be choosy. For one thing, I was still paying off the mortgage for the house my ex-wife and kids were still living in. It was of course the right thing to do.

My friend Ming had been going through similar hardships with family and business, and so had planned to move his family back to Hong Kong. Prior to doing this, he invited me over for tea. Whilst paying a visit to the bathroom, I noticed a book on a shelf called Harmonic Wealth. I started reading and couldn't stop. A worried Ming came knocking on the door - worried something terrible had happened! I assured him I was fine, but asked him about the book. He told me it was about the Law of Attraction and that could show me how to attract wealth in every area of my life. I had to borrow the book.

The Sanctuary of Healing

The next time I spoke to Ming I asked if he could point me in the direction of somebody who could do acupuncture, feeling that a spot of therapy could help me feel better about everything. I phoned the number he gave me but they said that I would be better off seeing a lady called Ann Marie James at the Sanctuary of Healing. I phoned Ann Marie and went to meet her. While I was waiting, a man with a really nice presence came into the waiting room and made eye contact with me. He came over and introduced himself to me as Tony Clarkson. He was the founder of The Sanctuary Of Healing. We only chatted briefly but. I thought he seemed like a really nice man and we really hit it off.

I went for my acupuncture. Ann Marie sat me down. She was a very calming lady. She asked me if I had ever taken drugs. I was ashamed to tell her that I had, but that I had never taken Heroin. I had to tell her I'd taken every other bloody drug out there though, and that I'd done so from an early age. She was blunt with me and told me I should technically be dead, but that she believed I was being kept alive for a reason. She told me I was giving out too much Yang, and that in order to balance things, I needed to bring some Yin into my life. I have to admit I felt a little confused. Nevertheless, I thanked Ann Marie for the treatment and went outside to my car. Without warning, I started sobbing. Everything was hitting me in some massive release - my childhood, what I'd done to my own family, the drugs, the choices I'd made… despite so much negativity, I was still here.

NLP & BNI

My solicitor, who had liquidated the bathroom company, happened to invite me to a network group called BNI during one of our talks. I talked to Dwayne about it and he said it would be a good idea to get some leads to sell photocopiers to. I went to the BNI breakfast meeting in my local area and met some amazing people, although I felt embarrassed standing up and saying, "Hi, my name's John Magee and I can save you money on your printing". I just had to remind myself that it was all helping to pay the bills. While sat in that first breakfast meeting, the first of two coincidental things happened. First, a lady called Amanda Meachin, a CEO of a local community and business partnership, stood up and announced that her partnership had just set up an extension for non-profit organisations to help their communities on Roman Road - the area of Blackburn I grew up in! Next, a lady called Imelda O'Keeffe stood up and introduced herself as an NLP Life Coach who could help people get what they want. I'd heard of NLP before… I flashed back

- Tony at the Sanctuary of Healing had also mentioned that he was an NLP master practitioner! The coincidences of late were speaking to me. I was intrigued to speak to both ladies and vowed to meet up with both.

Through chatting with Imelda, and later with Tony once more, a meeting had been arranged for me to meet with NLP 'guru', Chris Grimsley from NLP in The North West. Chris was just about to start teaching an NLP course in my area, as if by more of a coincidence, and invited me to sign up.

My chats with Amanda saw me really opening up to her about my upbringing on the estate she was now utilising as a community hub. I told her I was essentially an ex-con, and she said I was so much more than that - I was a role model. She invited me to speak at an event called Inspiring Communities, where I could engage young people to change their lives like I had done. Next thing I knew, I was on stage speaking to 100 young people. I was nervous, but spoke from the heart. It felt good.

Later that week I called one of my newest friends, Laura. We met up and had such a connection. She talked me into giving myself a pseudonym for my talks. We decided on Mister Consequence. The requests for talks came flooding in, then a friend called Deborah from www.mastery-path.com actually asked if I could speak on BBC television with world famous motivational and inspirational speaker, Richard McCann. I was in awe, and Mister Consequence was born. He wanted to help people.

Back to where it all began...

At the start of this 'timeline' I spoke to you about someone who I would go on to call my best friend. That person is David Dunn. He may have been a Premier League superstar at the time, but to me he was one of the most down to earth Blackburn with Darwen lads you could meet.

I had been speaking with David during this 'Mister Consequence' phase of my life about setting up a social enterprise called STREETS. I wanted to know if David would work with me to put together a mentoring pack based on our life experiences growing up as kids and teens in Blackburn with Darwen, Lancashire - one of the most deprived wards in the country. The mentoring pack would be designed to help support young people from socially deprived and challenging backgrounds similar to ours.

While spending months of my life drafting session plans designed to engage, mentor and support children, young people, families, schools and communities, I had an idea to write a session on RAOK - Random Acts Of Kindness. It all fit so perfectly - going right back to where it had all started between

David and I, supporting my wonderful friend Michelle, and subsequently honouring one of the kindest people in the world I could think of.

For me, kindness was a concept that anybody could apply, as Michelle always did, and therefore I believed it was important to make sure people knew just how much good they could do by engaging within its practices. Random or planned, acts of kindness would only ever have beneficiaries, and this was a ripple effect that I hoped would one day change the world.

In 2012, I formed a global kindness movement, it was, and still is, my mission to encourage people to take part in the Kindness Matters 30 Day challenge and experience the transformation that thousands of people from our global community swear by. I knew I could change the world, and I knew I could share with people the important message that Kindness Matters.

Why Kindness Matters

"All behaviour is learnt behaviour."

- NLP Presupposition

Why does Kindness Matter?

As I look back over some of the heartwarming stories within this book, I am filled with wonderful reflections regarding how those people who gave or carried out those acts of kindness will have felt at the time.

I encourage you, as the reader and as a Kindness Ambassador, to read the following statement to yourself and come up with three different possible sentence completions:

"I believe kindness matters because…"

If you are anything like me, feel free to write your completions in the section below for your own reference and affirmation:

✐ "I believe kindness matters because

...."

✐ "I believe kindness matters because

...."

✐ "I believe kindness matters because

...."

Whatever your completions were, I am sure you put them forward from the heart and that your affirmations would make a difference not only in your life, but in the lives of many others.

It's KIND of funny how we all practice kindness in our own way, based on the different ways in which we see the world. I am convinced that, when we begin to get a deeper understanding of WHY kindness matters, we can begin to make a massive difference in the world.

What I would like you to gain from this section of the book is this: As you read each story, I would like you to try to 'feel' what the giver may have been experiencing at the time of carrying out the act of kindness. When you have done that, I would then like you to imagine what it felt like to the person on the receiving end. Then, ask yourself WHY you believe this act of kindness was so important - why did it matter?

Because you and I are kindred spirits, I truly believe that you will notice a pattern here with the stories in this book. That pattern is that all the stories relate to something that I think a lot of people are missing a trick on, which is the act of GIVING.

I truly believe in the mantra that "it is in giving that we receive." Have a think about that. It ties in with my own personal mantra that "what you do comes back to you." I believe in all of this because kindness is a universal law! This is not to say that you or I or any members of our kindness community carry out daily acts of kindness in order to get something back, but it's just how the universe works. Whether you like it or not, when you do good deeds, good deeds tend to come back to you in many shapes and forms and that's a lovely feeling. A lot of the time, these things come back to you when you least expect them... How good is that?

Seriously, I have had so many seemingly random kind things happen to me when I have least expected them; whether it was when I was short on change, or being in receipt of a gift when it wasn't my birthday... I will bet my bottom dollar that such things have happened to you too, haven't they? Why? Because "what you do comes back to you" and because "it is in giving that you will receive."

Just imagine, as you and I continue to share our message with people, how by making kindness a part of a lifestyle and helping others understand WHY kindness matters, the difference we can make in the world. An extremely powerful way to make this happen is to do what many of the members do from our community, which is to share some of the stories you have read from the book with others in your life and maybe even use them to start an open discussion on the positive impact such things have on the giver and the receiver.

When you have had this discussion, ask that person: Why do you believe kindness matters?

Hopefully, you will get many pleasant answers in return.

Damsel in distress

Like most parents, during the week I have a lot of family commitments with my children – taking them to sports sessions, dance and drama activities and supporting them at their various and ever-growing list of new hobbies. I am always up against the clock and sometimes my angelic patience can be tested.

It was a Wednesday evening and my son and I were on our way to the local high school for football training, when on the way we spotted a young lady standing at the side of the road next to her car, which had presumably broken down. As you'd imagine, most drivers just drove straight past.

I pulled in front of the lady's car and put my hazard lights on - safety first! I jogged around to the lady's car (looking back now she may have thought I was trying to mug her)! I asked if she had broken down and she replied that she had but that her father was on his way to help. I said I'd like to help out anyway and at least wait with her for company.

KINDNESSMATTERS

You see, I believe that by performing daily acts of kindness, whether it's a daily compliment to someone, opening a door, helping someone in need or an act of charity, it makes you feel good. More importantly, it makes other people feel good. Remember "it's cool to be kind".

"If we all do one random act of kindness daily, we might just set the world in the right direction." - Martin Kornfeld

I love that frock!

It was a hot sunny day in July and I was working in my office. The place was like a ghost town as the offices my company rents are inside a school and it was the summer holidays. I was actually working on the new Random acts of kindness lesson plan to go into the STREETS Moral Education pack for the following term in September. I thought to myself, it's roasting outside so I'm going to treat myself to an ice lolly!

As I was walking to the local shop I took some time to listen to the birds tweeting and bumble bees buzzing. I enjoyed the feeling of the sun on my face and wondered if I may have the opportunity for any random act of kindness in the sun that day. I stopped off at a cash machine and out of the corner of my eye I saw a senior citizen walking across the road in my direction. She must have been 80+ (I hope she is not reading this).

As the lady got closer, I turned to her and said, "Oh my days what is that perfume you're wearing?" She quite rightfully looked shocked and taken aback. She answered by saying she wasn't sure what it was called. I told her that whatever it was it smelled lovely in the breeze and that it went really well with her summery frock! Well you should have seen the smile on her face! Considering I was standing next to a cash machine, my random act of kindness cost me nothing, yet the value was everything.

We all need to be shown kindness and we all need to express it. Acts of kindness connect us to one another.

What's that noise?

It was a Sunday morning, and like most dads up and down the country I had to get up for my son's football game. I had been working hard all over the North West for my role mentoring youngsters, and the long hours and high mileage were taking their toll.

I thought to myself that I'd have a little bit of a sleep-in as the game was not kicking off until 11am. Likewise, I left my kids in bed to have a well deserved rest. Just before 9am, I heard a commotion downstairs in the kitchen; pots clanging and pans banging. Ready to defend my fort, I stealthily crept downstairs. I needn't have worried, as the noise had been coming from the actions of my daughter, Millie. She had got up early that Sunday morning and, after waking me with the commotion, said to me, "Daddy, because I know how busy you are and how hard you have been working, I got up early and did all the dirty dishes in the sink and had a clean around in the kitchen as well!"

In carrying out this random act of kindness, my daughter actually made more of a mess in the kitchen than there was to start with, but that's really not the point.

That's my little girl.

To make a difference in someone's life, you don't have to be brilliant, rich, beautiful or perfect. You just have to care.

Say it with flowers

I, like many people, always have mixed emotions when visiting cemeteries and crematoriums following the passing of a loved one. Whenever I choose or need to visit one, it always gets me thinking about random acts of kindness.

One weekend, I'd taken my Mum to the cemetery to pay respects to her brother, my Uncle Robert, who had sadly passed the year before. I told Mum that I had bought an extra bunch of flowers to place on a grave that could do with a bit of a lift. I've done this before and some people get a bit funny about it, but that's the world we live in, and as long as you know you've done a good thing, that's all that matters. The person who has passed may not know about it, but think how the next loved one who visits will feel when they see this act of kindness. Even if they don't notice, the point of a random act of kindness is that it is carried out with indiscriminate love, and I always think this story is a great example of that.

> *"Every thought, every emotion, every word spoken, every action is a seed sown."* - Steven Claysen

Comfort food

I am forever sharing the power of random acts of kindness with the students I teach and the groups I mentor in my role. With education the way it is, random acts of kindness in school can be so important, and so I am similarly always badgering my students to think about the random acts of kindness they can carry out for their peers, teachers and staff.

One particular week, one of my students shared with our group that he was at home the night before and his mum was full of a cold in bed. He had remembered about the random acts of kindness sessions so he went upstairs to his savings jar and took some money to take to the local shop. Whilst there, he bought his mum a Pot Noodle. Now personally, I'd rather eat cardboard, and I'm sure it wasn't the nutrition this boy's mum

KINDNESSMATTERS

was craving during her sickness, but how lovely it must have felt for her to receive this thought, if not the gift itself?

How beautiful a day can be when kindness touches it.

Super size the random acts of kindness

One Friday afternoon I was lucky to grab some time with an old friend who wanted to chat to me about setting up a project for local homeless people. As we made our way into a well known fast food burger place, my friend gave me her order and went to find some comfortable seats where we could catch up. I'd already decided to pay for her meal, given how lovely I thought her homelessness project was, but I wondered if there were any other random acts of kindness I could do that day.

As I placed our order, I decided that the next person who walked in behind me, I'd pay for their order, also! As a result, a gentleman who placed an order for a chocolate milkshake got a very nice surprise when he heard me say to the server, "I'll pay for this gentleman, thank you!"

The guy in question thanked me and laughed, saying he'd wished he'd have ordered the entire menu instead!

Let your kindness be like the rain, that cares not
whom it falls on.

I see you!

Last year, I found myself lucky enough to be working over in Cambodia, and I found myself in a vegetarian café which I had previously visited and loved. As I was waiting for my food and taking in the ambience, I began to people watch. I noticed in the not too distant view, a young lady doing her best to shovel a load of muck and dirt from her garden that had been dumped from a neighboring building site. I noticed lots of people walk past her, but nobody helped, even though it was clear she was struggling in the heat.

I thought it would be a perfect opportunity to carry out a random act of kindness "Cambodian style"! I left my table in the café, and walked straight across to the lady and took her shovel from her. In hindsight, she could have got scared and hit me with it, but I didn't give her chance to think as I started shoveling through the dirt for her, helping her move it. Though I speak none of the local language, I managed to communicate with this lady through gestures and smiles, and together we made a great team! I noticed on my walk back to the café that loads of people had been watching me. Perhaps they'll all be inspired and take similar action one day.

When an act of kindness touches another soul, all humanity becomes stronger.

Paying it forward

I work in a petrol station, and I always remember a gentleman coming into the station one quiet evening and chatting with me about random acts of kindness as he gathered some purchases. I don't remember how that conversation started, but I remember thinking it was cool to chat about that kind of thing.

A few months later, also at work, it was a busy day when I heard a baby screaming and a child crying somewhere at the back of the shop. Both youngsters were with a lady. As she made her way to the counter, it was quite clear that she was upset and distressed herself. I was polite and did my best to cheer her up while the kids were crying. She said the baby was crying because it had not been fed and that she had walked to the station to put money on the gas and electric meter. As she started to rummage through her bag she began to break down and cry, as she realised she had left her purse at home and had no money on her. I felt so sorry for her.

I remembered what the gentlemen from months ago had said about random acts of kindness, and I told the lady to just give me a minute. I went into the back office at the station and got my last £10 out of my purse and put £5 on each utility key for her. She was sobbing and saying that she would come back and pay me. I told her not to, and asked that she 'pay if forward' instead. This way, I hope she can feel the same good feeling that I did when helping out someone in distress.

Your kindness could light up another's life.

Kindness platform - Dominic Ashton

A while ago I was waiting on a station platform, ready waiting for my train to London to play a rugby match. Prior to the train arriving, a member of platform staff began to pace the platform, asking if anyone could help her with an emergency medical situation. Immediately, our team's two physios stepped forward to help. The staff member told them that a woman had collapsed and had stopped breathing.

The lads raced down the platform to the lady in distress. I followed and watched in awe as they worked with the staff team to carry out CPR until the lady began to slowly but steadily respond.

I know that carrying out any act of first aid isn't exactly a random act of kindness, but I just wanted to give these guys a shout-out, as it's inspired me to get myself on a first aid course.

After all, what if our lads wouldn't have been there?

When we all help one another, everybody wins.

We love Random Acts of Kindness

The world is such a small place when you come to think about it. I am a big fan of social media as it helps me reach out to so many people on so many levels. It's a good method to spread random acts of kindness.

Over the years, I have met some lovely people via social media who share a common goal with me, which is to spread positivity everywhere they go.

The first lady I met on Instagram was Primrose from a group called 5 Acts a Day. She does some amazing random acts of kindness by placing positive sticky notes around places for people and hosting various retreats and workshops, which I am looking forward to being part of in the future. Primrose is just one of the many people on social media doing positive things. I urge you to find those people and let others know.

For me personally, I am honored to be in a position to share the love, and privileged to do what I do for a living to inspire and motivate people to do the same thing and to follow their dreams. This message is dedicated to you and lots of others who carry out daily acts of kindness and Random acts of kindness Keep up the good work. It's cool to be kind!

Umbrella, ella, ella! - Vince Wilkinson

I was about to make my way to the bus stop when I noticed the heavens were about to open, so I quickly grabbed my umbrella as I did not like the thought of getting soaked. I made my way to the bus stop slowly with my walking stick. The reason I have to take public transport and why I have a walking stick is because a couple of years ago, I was in a severe road traffic accident, where I got hit on my motorbike and shattered my pelvis and my femur. While it hurt, and it's inconvenient, the accident has made me grateful, and I now appreciate the simple things in life a lot more, like nature and being kind.

I digress! I made it into town, and the rain was starting to come down heavily. Through the raindrops, I noticed an elderly lady getting wet while walking in the rain with her shopping. I wanted to help, so I walked over and put the umbrella over her head and asked her where she was going. She told me she was headed to the train station, right the way across town. I insisted I walked with her the whole way, keeping the umbrella on her at all times.

As we walked, we talked about how it does not take much to take the time to be kind and compassionate to people, and the lady said the world needed more people like me! Well, I don't know about that, but the sentiment made me feel good. I told her to keep the umbrella.

In memory of Paula Walsh - Rest in peace

In my former life, I worked for a local paper. In a department full of women. We were outnumbered!

There was one particular woman by the name of Paula, who I liked a lot. She was such a kind soul and always had something positive to say. She was incredibly witty, and one of the things that drew me to her was her charisma and her beautiful voice. She had told me once that she sang in a choir. I once even had the pleasure of getting to hear her sing.

We lost touch, of course, over the years after I left that office, but I was still devastated when I found out she had died of cancer.

As people tend to do as a first port of reflection, I found her Facebook page (we'd become Facebook friends some years previously) and sought to post a message to her family. It was while looking at her Facebook 'wall' that I spotted the following message, posted by Paula herself some days earlier...

I gave my cup of tea to an old lady while waiting in the radiotherapy clinic today. She had travelled nearly two hours to get there and had to wait at least another two when she arrived. She needed that cuppa much more than me.
A Kindness Ambassador to the end.
Paula Walsh - R.I.P

"No one is born hating another person because of the colour of their skin, or his background, or his religion. People learn to hate, and if they can learn to hate, they can be taught to love, for love comes more naturally to the human heart than its opposite."

- Nelson Mandela

Random Acts Of Kindness!

Is it just me, or are they quite random?

Or, think of it this way... what if the random acts of kindness we experience/ are presented with are indeed merely beautifully wrapped coincidences for us to take full advantage of?

Whether they are truly random or not, in this section of the book, what I am hoping you will take from the stories of RAOK (Random Acts Of Kindness) is that the opportunities to do them can and will present themselves to you on a D.A.I.L.Y basis.

Let me ask you some questions.

Do you believe kindness should be actioned for all beings?

Is it equally as important to be kind to animals as well as to people too?

I am hoping that my questions will encourage you to explore lots of personal views. Although we all know what kindness is, sometimes we action it in different ways and it can be easy to lose sight of who (or what) can really benefit. I challenge you to see kindness through the eyes of another being.

RANDOM ACTS OF KINDNESS

One of my great mentors through my own reading, Dr Wayne Dyer, famously said, "If you change the way you look at things, the things you look at change." I will never forget the day I read this quote for the first time and how it made me look at how I practice my D.A.I.L.Y kindness in a totally different manner.

Since forming my global Kindness movement in 2012, I have done all I can to protect and promote the well-being of all creatures. If I see a spider in the bathroom, I will set it free. If a wasp flew in through the window right now, I would want to run away! But, then I would still do what I could with a glass and a beer mat in order to capture it in order to set it back into its habitat (hopefully without it stinging me)!

What I have found over the years is that nothing bad ever comes from carrying out acts of kindness. The key word here is ACTS. You will certainly always be given lots of opportunities to action random acts of kindness in your D.A.I.L.Y life, but the question is, will you take the time to notice and to say "yes" and take action? I will be talking a lot more in depth about this later on in the book and hopefully what I share with you will help you do just that when you commit to your Kindness Matters 30 Day Challenge.

What I love about the stories in this book is that there is a real 'mixed bag' of people involved and their values differ wonderfully. I like to put myself in their shoes and become consciously aware and empathically connected to what they will have felt and experienced as they performed their acts of kindness. I am convinced that when we get a deeper understanding of how our kind acts can have a massive impact in all lives, then we begin to start the process to deepen our awareness of empathy and compassion for all beings - not just those with which we are personally familiar.

"Every individual matters. Every individual has a role to play. Every individual makes a difference." - Jane Goodall

My random act of kindness for today was that I went to my kids' school and donated the old uniforms that my kids no longer fit into. They were of good quality so it made sense, as not every family can afford even those essentials.
Araceli Chavez

I saw a man in the street just before Christmas. He had on a leather coat, which was torn to shreds. He had dreadlocks and they looked matted and dirty. He was going around asking people for money. I didn't talk to him at first.

Later on, when I had finished my shopping, I noticed he was standing alone and not talking to anybody. He looked sad. I decided to talk to him. He was clutching some change so I felt happier that somebody had given him some money, but this man then told me that no shops would let him in to buy any food because he looked dirty and scruffy. I could have just gone into the shops on his behalf to buy him something, but I wanted to do more than that. I asked him to come into a shop with me, as I calmly told the staff that they could not refuse service to a paying customer. They looked embarrassed, and I hope it will make them think in future.

The man was so appreciative and polite. It was a massive reminder to me about how unkind it is to judge people on how they look.
Rachel Lalas

I have been working some serious hours lately, including a part time job I have in a bar at the weekend. It's been good to have some extra money coming in. One day, a good friend called me in tears from her own place of work. She was angry and confused that she had been underpaid for the month, and told me that money was so tight for her at the moment as a result. She had paid off her bills, as with the start of every month, but she didn't have enough left to buy her beloved dog any food as a result of the accounting error. I comforted her over the phone and told her I would come round later on when she had finished work.

The minute I stepped foot out of my door, I went to the nearest supermarket and bought my friend (well, her dog) a load of dog food and doggy treats. I knocked on the door but there was no

KINDNESSMATTERS

answer, as my friend was still at work. So, I posted the doggy treats through her letterbox and left the dog food by her front door.

I bet when she got home she must have thought I was barking mad!
Leona Jane Magee

Sharing random acts of kindness across the pond

The power of social media.
Like most people, I am present on most social media channels, and I use these to help spread the message that Kindness Matters.

Instagram is my favourite, and it's there where something amazing happened to me recently. Amid all the like-minded people I connect with on there, my favourite was connecting with Dennis and Herazee. Even though they were thousands of miles away in Florida, USA, I felt a strong connection through our shared images and messages. I contacted them to arrange a Skype call.

Before I knew it, the call was in full flow with chat and laughter, and these two beautiful souls had almost instantly signed up to the Kindness Matters 30 Day challenge - keen to take my vision global.

When we finished the call, I wished Dennis and Herazee a Happy Christmas and New Year as I was off on my travels to Cambodia. Before I went though, I sent them both a copy of of my favourite book along with some other spiritual pieces I knew they'd like. When I got back from my trip, I found that Dennis and Herazee had contacted me with a message to say it was one of the nicest things they had ever experienced. The picture they sent to prove this really made my day!

Dennis & Herazee - Florida USA

You will never regret being kind.

Negative to a positive

It was a Monday morning, and I was mentoring a group of Year Ten learners from a school in Burnley, Lancashire.

As with most Monday mornings, not all of the students were in the mood for learning.

My colleague Craig and I were due to escort our students to the local Youth Zone for a session. Craig walked the boys while I followed on in the car. Upon arrival, I parked in the local car park and then joined everybody ready for their morning mentoring.

After the session, I noticed out of the window that a traffic warden was putting a ticket on my car, I felt my Moody Meter drop instantly to a number 1, and became aware of an overwhelming emotion of negativity rising. As I ran out the door, I began to think what I could do stop this negative feeling. Then it came to me - do the opposite! So, instead of being hostile, be polite.

As I approached the traffic warden, he said, "Sorry pal, you've not got a permit". He probably expected a verbal attack, but I just admitted to him that it was fair and that there was little I could do. I said, "You're only doing your job, mate". He looked really shocked and actually a little relieved. This instantly made me feel better.

I felt better too, and wanted to continue this feeling. So. I decided to make someone's day. I went out and bought a lottery ticket, and found a scrap of paper to scrawl the following words:

"Sorry for the fright, hope you win the lottery!"

With that, I placed the ticket and the note inside the yellow and black plastic wallet that my parking ticket had been so lovingly placed in earlier in the day. I then stuck the wallet onto the windscreen of a random car. I knew that the initial shock would make the driver feel negative, but that the positive that would follow would be absolutely enormous in return.

My only regret is that I never got to see their face when they opened it!.

Never get tired of doing little things for others. Sometimes those little things occupy the biggest part of their heart.

> *"Serve the needs of others and all your own needs will be fulfilled."* -Dr Wayne Dyer

Why did the hedgehog cross the road?

You really can't beat a lovely sunny afternoon. When I am at work on days like that, I do like to get out of the office every now and then as there is no natural light between those four walls. This particular afternoon, I went to pick up some lunch, and whilst I was mainly preoccupied with my sandwich, I noticed in the not too far distance something coming out of the bushes. As I looked closer, making its way onto a busy road was a little hedgehog! So beautiful, but I feared the worst! I ran into the road and signalled for the traffic to stop - God knows what these people thought was going on. As the cars stopped, I ran to the hedgehog and picked him up (carefully), before placing him across the road in a thick bush, which is hopefully where he was trying to get to.

I believe we should show loving kindness to animals, too.
Kelly Fletcher

Children's Raok

Is it just me, or is there something magical about witnessing a child or young person carrying out an act of kindness?

Can you imagine how I felt, in that case, when I had the privilege during my career to be 'out on the road' for three years, working with hundreds of young people from around the North West of England to promote the Kindness Matters 30 Day Challenge?

There is an old comedic saying, "I love kids, but I couldn't eat a full one." There's some seriousness in this when we think of the fact that some kids these days are a lot to stomach, to say the least! Teenagers, in particular, don't get the best press. This has never stopped me wanting to work with them, though - they need it the most, I think!

For the record, we have all been kids and teenagers at one point, and it can be one of the most challenging times in your life in making the transition from childhood to adulthood. What I learned from ALL the young people I had the pleasure of working with on the road out in schools and colleges was that they were all surprisingly open with kindness. In some ways, they absorbed the concept like sponges, and especially liked the Wayne Dyer quote, "If you change the way you look at things, the things you look at change." I indeed began to change the way I perceived young people in terms of their kindness by witnessing and having them share with me the kindness that they were applying each day within their communities.

KINDNESSMATTERS

I recall sharing this information with our Kindness Community and many members shared something very precious with me which I feel is going to add real value to your kindness journey as you read this book. But first, let me ask you some questions:

What was the best story about kindness that you ever remember hearing or reading?

What was it about that story that inspired you or spoke to you?

It's fair to say that since the dawn of civilisation and since we all first sat around making fire, we have always learned from stories we have heard. Well, this is what members of our Kindness Community were telling me - they had learned from those they looked up to, such as parents. With this in mind, they felt compelled to pass on their learnings to their children (or the little ones of those they loved). So, perhaps the way to spread kindness isn't just to do it; it's to tell people about it too.

Share your stories, or those that you have heard yourself and get into conversations with your kids. Ask questions, especially before that child goes to bed, as the good feelings the sharing will evoke will make for a great night of sleep and the possibility of some pretty inspirational dreams.

Let me finish this section by quoting a famous pop song... "I believe the children are our future..." Think about it!

"I believe the children are our future. Teach them well and let them lead the way. Show them all the beauty they possess inside."

- Linda Creed

Jade & Beth - Age 12

I would like to share this random act of kindness with you and tell you about what I chose to do for young people in my community.

A lot of the kids from my school don't have much and are a lot less fortunate than other kids.

I love reading and had heard at school that a lot of kids were struggling with literacy..

I got talking to my friend Beth and told her I had an idea to help children get better at reading. Beth asked me what the idea was, and I told her I wanted to set up a reading club for the younger children in the school.

We worked out that we could run the club every Friday, so we set up our Random Acts of Kindness Reading Club, and there are so many kids that come and look up to us as positive role models while we read together.

We have looked at creative writing in the books we read and explored how to have confidence reading out loud.

We find it so rewarding giving back and watching kids achieve!

A little spark of kindness can put a colossal burst of sunshine into someone's day.

KINDNESS MATTERS

Joe - Age 11

I was on my way home from school on the bus and there was an elderly man sitting in front of me. We had been learning about how small acts of kindness can have a big positive role in people's lives so I sat next to the gentleman and told him he had a nice hat. He smiled at me and it felt great. I got off at my next stop and thought that didn't cost much but the smile on his face was priceless.

Natasha - Age 11

I was walking home close to a man I'd seen around a lot, and he was carrying what looked like heavy shopping bags. I was shocked to see him fall down, so I ran over to help him. I asked some other adults to help me too and we walked him to his house. His wife was so upset but so grateful, and actually offered me some money for helping. I couldn't take the money - that's not what being kind is about. Plus I told his wife that my mum would kill me if I accepted money for something like that.

I CAN be KIND therefore I WILL be KIND.

Danny

It was a nice hot sunny day down on the Promenade in Blackpool, and whilst I was walking along the seafront with my mates, I noticed across the road a lady with a screaming baby in a pram. The lady looked a bit worried and seemed to be searching for something on the floor. I noticed that the baby had thrown the dummy out of its pram, so I left my mates, crossed the road safely and ran over to pick up the dummy off the floor. I cleaned it as best as I could and then offered it to the lady.

The lady actually snapped at me because she hadn't seen what I'd done and just thought I was going to hassle her (us teenagers get a bad reputation). When I explained what had happened though, she smiled and looked both relieved and thankful. I felt great, and within a few seconds the baby stopped crying thanks to its returned dummy! As I ran back to my mates, I shouted to the lady that I'd just done a random act of kindness. When she looked puzzled, I said, "Random Act of Kindness". She smiled and waved, and I couldn't wait to tell everyone how good my random act of kindness made me feel.

It only takes one person and one act of kindness to inspire others and create change.

Lucas and his Lollipop

One of the many great gifts random acts of kindness brings is teaching your children how to practice daily acts of kindness – planned or random. My kids think I am mad when I tell them some of the random acts of kindness I carry out, but they do take the concept on board and to heart.

It was coming to the end of the school term and my son, Lucas, was coming to the end of his Primary School experience. He said to me one morning on the school run, "You know what, Dad we should do a random act of kindness for Aunty Anne the Lollipop Lady, because she does such a good job keeping everyone safe on that busy road near school".

I was delighted with the thought and the reasoning, so we took a quick detour to the local shop and picked up some chocolates for Aunty Anne the Lollipop Lady!

Aunty Anne loved the chocolates, but perhaps we should have bought her lollipops?

Michael - Age 13

Yes, I open doors for people and say "please" and "thank you", but I had always felt that I could do more. I had heard about Random acts of kindness and was keen to get involved! As a result, I created a poster to encourage people to "Keep Calm and do random acts of kindness" I hope it works!

A simple act of kindness has the power to change a life.

Year 8 Fundraiser Car Wash

Last year, we lost our teacher at school to Cancer. We know it's only a small thing to do, but we staged a charity car wash at school and donated all the money raised to the charity that

KINDNESSMATTERS

supported our teacher and her family through her illness. We think she will have been proud of us.

Believe in the magic of kindness.

Kayleigh - Age 12

We should always value our parents and carers. Early this morning, I went to the shop with my own money and bought a thank you card for my mum and stepdad – just because. I also bought some chocolate for them. It was a nice surprise for them, and that's what a random act of kindness should be.

How beautiful a day can be when kindness touches it.

Charlie and Mitchell - Age 12

Me and my friend Mitchell were walking past Blockbuster – a local shop that had recently closed down. Outside, we noticed a homeless man with his dog. Mitchell had initially wanted to get some sweets from the shop down the road, but he told me that he didn't feel like it anymore, and instead took out his money and went in the direction of the bakery. I followed him and we bought the homeless man a pie and a bottle of water. We walked up to the homeless man and gave him the food and drink. He was so grateful and kept saying, "God bless you". We're not really religious, but this was really nice to hear and we felt really happy having helped someone in need.

Skye - Age 12

My random act of kindness happened yesterday when my auntie cancelled babysitting at short notice, meaning that my mum had nobody to look after the baby when she went to work. I told her that I'd babysit instead!

On top of that, before my mum left to go to work, I went out to the shop and bought her a chocolate milkshake (her favourite) and a Toblerone. I told her I hoped it would make her night at work a little bit more fun!

Every new day is a chance to change your life.

Alanya - Age 13

On Thursday evening after school, I sat alone blocking out the idiotic immature teenagers at the back of the bus with my music. A few stops before where I usually get off the bus, a gorgeous old lady wiggled her way through all the passengers. I spotted her frightened face, looking around at her intimidating surroundings. There was no place for her to sit. She struggled with her shopping as she walked, and so I stood and offered her my seat. She refused, but I insisted for her to sit. I took her bags and stood there watching her sit down. I placed the bags at her feet. She smiled at me.

My heart started beating really fast. She was so cute. Her smile could light up the bus. It was one of those smiles that you can't forget, and I want to see smiles like that every day from now on!

Wherever there is a human being, there is an opportunity for kindness.

Callum - Age 12

I was on my way to school one Tuesday morning and I saw an opportunity to do a random act of kindness. There was a fire engine coming up the road and there was a lady struggling to get out of the side road in her car as a result, so I thought I would guide her out safely onto the road. I was mindful it could make me late for school but I thought it was a good deed for the day so I'd take the risk. With my help, the lady pulled out of the road, smiled and waved at me before driving off. I went school feeling good for the rest of the day.

Never underestimate the power of a simple act of kindness. Your act might be the added lift that someone needs to go from falling to flying.

Kerrie - Age 13

It was a Sunday evening when I was feeling in a bubbly mood and wanted to take a trip down to the shops. What happened next is something that usually happens to me because I'm clumsy, but I watched as a fellow shopper accidently knocked everything off the shelves whilst trying to reach a loaf of bread. Cringe! Of course, the shopkeeper was angry and looked as if he was about to murder someone as a result of the incident that had just happened. I didn't want the lady to get into trouble so I stepped up and took the blame and offered to help clean up. The lady was so thankful, and I felt as if a big chunk of my heart was warming up! I was glad I helped her, because I know what it feels like to be on the other side of that situation.

A generous heart, a kind speech, and a life of service and compassion are the things that renew humanity.

Chelsea - Age 10
A £20 note fell out of a woman's pocket whilst she was running past me. My cousin told me to keep it but I said no because it wasn't mine to keep. I ran after the woman and gave her back her money. She was very grateful and thanked me.

Brandon - Age 11
When my mum was ill, I made her something to eat and a cup of tea. She also likes chocolate, so I got my money, went to the shop and bought her some of her favourite chocolates. It made us both feel better.

Maahnoor - Age 10
I was walking down the street and I saw an old lady struggling with her shopping so I helped her to carry it and walked with her to her house.

KINDNESSMATTERS

Enoch - Age 10

I was in town near McDonalds when I saw a homeless man sitting outside. I had £10 spending money so I gave the homeless man £5 of it.

Chris - Age 12

I went to the shop to buy some bread for my dad. I saw this old lady in front of me buying her milk. She was 50p short so I gave her the 50p and the smile on her face was massive.

Cory - Age 12

It was a Sunday morning and I was playing football with my team when after the game I noticed a man was struggling with his car which was stuck in the mud. I said to my friend, Jenson, and his Dad, that we should go and help the man who was clearly going nowhere and making a bigger hole with the tyres in the mud. We helped him and he pipped his horn to say thank you!

Kindness, like a boomerang, always returns.

Taylor - Age 15

I was walking along the road with my friends when suddenly my heart dropped. I saw an elderly woman struggling with all her shopping. I ran over to help. I thought my mates would help but they walked off instead.

I told the lady to be careful not to hurt herself if she was carrying a lot of bags in the future. She smiled and couldn't stop saying thank you. Then she went into her purse and held out some coins for me. I rejected the kind offer and instead told her to have a lovely day, before I turned around and went home.

Later that day I told people about what had happened and they couldn't believe I turned down the money. There's nothing wrong with being kind, and if you're kind you will always get it back some way or another. Live life to the full but always be kind whatever you do.

Melissa - Age 11

When I went to Stanley Park with my mum, we walked past a lady with a scraggy little dog. The lady threw a ball with one of those plastic things you throw for your pets. The ball hurled through the air and landed in a water fountain. The lady struggled with getting the ball back, so I told my mum I was going to do a random act of kindness and help her out.

KINDNESSMATTERS

I ran over, took my shoes and socks off and climbed into the fountain. I probably looked like an idiot, but at least I did a random act of kindness!

We rise by lifting others.

Abbie - Age 10

I was in Barrow In Furness (Cumbria) with my family, and whilst we were in town we decided to go and grab a sandwich and sit in a park somewhere.

This man sat next to us who had just come out of a sports shop with six or seven massive bags full of sports gear. As he was sat on the bench he began to get some of his items out to look at.

His phone began to ring and he got up and set off to walk away, forgetting one of his bags. I quickly ran over to get the bag, picked it up and ran after him to hand it over. He was thankful and even gave me a fiver!

One kind act can change someone's entire day.

We all need to be shown kindness and we all
need to express it. Acts of kindness connect
us to one another.

HINTS & TIPS

Within this section of the book, I am hoping that you will find more kindness hints and tips than you can shake a stick at.

As most people in our Kindness Community know, I do like my quotes! With that in mind, let me say this: "If it doesn't challenge you, it won't change you!" I remember hearing this quote for the first time when I did a parachute jump for charity. I also remember that it took my mother weeks to get the stains out of my underwear afterwards, but that's another story!

Now, I am certainly not asking you to challenge yourself by throwing yourself out of an aircraft from 16,500 feet like I did! What I am going to encourage you to do instead is to read through the hints and tips in this section and highlight any 30 acts of kindness that you personally think would be challenging for you to do. Tell yourself for each one that you CAN do that you WILL do it. At the end of the day, this is YOUR kindness journey and anyway, you can journal this and challenging yourself along the way is good for your reflection on the good work you are doing for others.

For me personally, I believe that we learn so much about ourselves when we work outside of our comfort zone. As one of my good friends said to me recently, "The comfort zone is where the dreams go to die." Just imagine how utterly amazing you will feel when you apply an act of kindness that you have never done before and as you watch the magic unfold for everyone involved! How good it that?

Please do not get me wrong; there will be lots of kindness hints and tips within this section which are very basic and easy to do, like holding open doors, giving compliments, picking up pieces of litter you did not drop etc, and I am not saying for one minute that these small things are less important - they are most certainly not! If back to basics is where you need to start on your journey, just do it. There is no such thing as a small act of kindness.

On a final note, if there are any acts of kindness that you regularly continue to do, such as always picking up litter as suggested, then don't forget to share them with people in order to inspire them to do the same. My hope is that from this section of the book, you will find kindness hints and tips that you may have never even thought about before and that they will excite you with the prospect of applying them.

Enjoy, my fellow Kindness Ambassadors.

Do something today that your future self
will thank you for.

Community

- Put your next door neighbour's bin out for rubbish or recycling collection

- Hold a jumble sale with all your old toys and clothes and then donate the money to a local children's centre or project

- Tell a police officer that you are grateful for them keeping your community safe

- Tell somebody who collects rubbish or picks litter that they are doing a good job for the communityEvery day, list three things you are grateful for

- Leave some credit at a parking station for the next person

- Volunteer at a nursing home

- Leave a pound coin on the bus

- Say thank you to a caretaker, security guard or public transport driver

- Give a compliment to a lollipop person

- Leave a pound coin in a shopping trolley

- Volunteer at a local community group

- Donate food out of your cupboards to a food bank

HINTS AND TIPS

- Leave a copy of your favourite book on a bench with a nice message inside it on a sticky note for the person who finds it to read

- Make bacon sandwiches for the dustbin men

- When eating sweets or chewing gum while travelling on public transport, offer one to any people you make eye contact with

- Buy your neighbour something nice for their garden

- Become a community volunteer

"Service to others is the rent you pay for your room here on earth." - Muhammad Ali

- Leave one of your favourite books on public transport

- Buy a gift voucher and donate it to someone you respect from your community

- Help a parent who may be struggling with a pram

- Give a Lotto ticket or scratchcard to a complete stranger

- Bake muffins for your local doctors and surgery staff

- Offer to wash your neighbour's car

- Help someone struggling with heavy bags

HINTS AND TIPS

- Give up some of your time to volunteer for a local community group or charity

- Give your postman a thank you card

- Help the elderly

- Donate a first aid kit to a local community group

- Donate a pair of decent quality old shoes to a shoe bank

- Give someone a tissue who's crying in public and offer to listen

- Let a member of your community know you respect the work that they do to help others

- Buy your neighbour's cat or dog a packet of food or some tasty treats

- Buy a bottle of chilled water on a hot day and give it to someone who looks thirsty

- Take time to have a conversation with a senior citizen and make it your mission to find out lots about them

- Let somebody in a queue go before you

- Save all your change and donate it to a small charity that does not get a lot of support

- Say hello to everyone you pass in the street

KINDNESSMATTERS

- Write a message on social media, encouraging everybody to become part of www.kindnessmatters.me

- Offer to walk the dogs at an animal shelter

- Take a cake or some sweet treats to your local fire station

Family

- Give a family member a hug

- Set the dinner table at home

- Make your parents or breakfast in bed

- Tidy up around the house

- Put your dirty clothes in the laundry

- Design or buy a gift for a family member

- Ask a member of your family how their day has been

- Make your mum, dad or carer a cup of tea without them asking

"Life is short, but there is always time for courtesy."
- Ralph Waldo Emerson

- Phone your Grandma or Granddad and tell them you are grateful that they are your grandparents

- Babysit for any new parents in your life

- Get up early and tidy the house before anyone gets up

Friends

- Write a poem and give it to your colleague

- Look for an opportunity to give a friend or a work colleague a lift to wherever they're going

- Give an old but good quality piece of jewellery to a friend

- Tell a friend something that you like about them

- Give someone you know a hug

- Ask a friend's parent how their day has been

- Call a friend and ask them if they need help with anything

- Help somebody pack up their shopping at the supermarket

- Try to make sure every person in a group conversation feels included

- Randomly text a handful of friends and tell them how grateful you are for them being such a good friend to you

- Choose to share something with a friend

- Tell one of your fitness fanatic friends that their hard work is paying off

- Record a video message for friends or family who live far away

- Give your friend a hug for no reason

School

- Write a poem and give it to your favourite teacher

- Tell the dinner lady at school that the food tastes great

- Tidy up after someone else's lunch

- Help the teacher hand out the books

- Offer to help pupils who are lost

- Return lost property

- No running in the corridor

- No pushing in the canteen area

- Talk to someone at school that you haven't talked to before

- Return a coat to a pupil or member of staff

- Say thank you to the school caretaker/cleaner

- If another pupil is upset to see if they are ok

- No pushing when leaving the classroom

- Make new pupils feel welcome

HINTS AND TIPS

- Help a teacher with their books or equipment

- Organise a school raffle and donate all the money to the school

- Pick up a piece of litter you didn't drop and put it in the bin

- Hold the door open for someone

"How beautiful a day can be when kindness touches it!"
- George Elliston

- Offer other pupils a drink

- Ask the teacher how their day has been

- Read to another pupil in class

- Design a thank you card

- Sharpen the pencils in the classroom

- Use your manners with the canteen staff

- Don't say mean words or use nasty gestures

- Wash your hands before and after break times

- Give a teacher compliment

- Bring in a piece of fruit for your teacher

KINDNESSMATTERS

HINTS AND TIPS

- Thank your teachers regularly for helping you get a good education

- Help one of your friends who is struggling with their homework

- Tell a teacher that you enjoyed their lesson

- Email or write a letter to a teacher who has made a difference in your life

- Do not shout out in class

- Bring a spare pen into school and give it to that one person who always forgets their own

- Share classroom equipment

- At a local sporting event, cheer for the losing team

- Apologise when you know you got something wrong

- Give something you make in a technology class to your favourite teacher

- Give someone you know a hug

- Make or draw a picture for your headteacher or a teacher

- Offer to tie somebody's tie or shoelaces

Environment

Collect all your plastic carrier bags and recycle them

- Organise a Clean Up Litter campaign

- Turn off electrical items when not in use

> *"Be the change that you want to see in the world."*
> - Mahatma Gandhi

- Create a bug house

- Reduce, Re-use, Recycle

- Turn off the water tap after washing your hands

- Plant something

- Put a spare carrier bag in your car to collect recycling or rubbish when you are out and about

- Turn off the water when brushing your teeth

- Water your neighbour's plants

- Reuse your carrier bags

- Pick up a piece of litter that was not yours and put it in the bin

- Tidy up after someone else's lunch

KINDNESSMATTERS

Random acts of kindness (RAOK)

- Pay for somebody behind you at a toll road

- Do a chore for someone without them knowing

- Buy a packet of crisps or a bar of chocolate in a local shop and ask the shopkeeper to pay it forward and give it to the next person that comes in to buy something

- Phone your local takeaway and when you pay for your order, pay for an extra item such as garlic bread, and ask for it to be added to the order for the next customer

- When dining out, leave a written message telling your waiter/waitress that their service was outstanding

- Pay for somebody's drink at a bar without telling them

- Give a helping hand to a random stranger in need

- Forgive someone who has hurt your feelings

- Sing songs at a nursing home (Christmas is a good time)

- Apologise to somebody even when you think they're in the wrong

- When buying a ticket to a gig, buy an extra ticket and donate it on social media

- Leave a pound coin in a bus stop

KINDNESSMATTERS

- Buy a kite and give it to a parent and child playing in the park

- Write a letter or an email of appreciation to a person who has made a difference in your life

- Compliment someone on the outfit they are wearing

- Thank somebody you are talking to for having a lovely smile

- Give a hug to somebody who is upset

- When visiting a lost relative or friend at the cemetery or crematorium, bring an extra bunch of flowers and place them on a grave

- Make your parents or partner breakfast in bed

"Happiness is like perfume; you can't pour it on somebody else without getting a few drops of it on yourself."
- James Van Der Zee

- Pay a compliment to the next receptionist you talk to

- Donate a piece of your favourite clothing to somebody who has always liked it

- Give up your seat on a bus or a train for somebody else

KINDNESSMATTERS

HINTS AND TIPS

- Leave a nice tip at a restaurant

- Share your headphones with your music playing when on public transport

- Choose and write a nice postcard and send it to someone

- Send a hand-written letter to someone in the Armed Forces

- Buy a bar of chocolate and hand it to a random person on your journey

- Register to become an organ donor

- Bake a cake for someone and decorate it in a meaningful way

- Give up your time to complete customer feedback after somebody serves you in a shop or restaurant

- Hold the door open for someone

- Be polite to a random telesales person who phones you when it is not the best of times

- Use your manners - say please and thank you more often

- Give someone a compliment

- Send flowers to somebody – just because

- Bake cakes or biscuits and give them away

HINTS AND TIPS

- Leave a bar of chocolate in the locker at your local gym as a reward for their good workout

- Bring doughnuts to work for your colleagues to enjoy during the day

- Compliment a parent on how well-behaved their child is

- Compliment someone to his or her boss

- Leave a magazine behind for someone else to read at the coffee shop, the doctor's office or on a train

- Buy an inspirational book for somebody who you think may need it Kindness Matters would be a good choice

- Bring a security guard a hot cup of coffee – maybe even throw in some biscuits!

- Talk to someone at work that you haven't talked to before

- Tell someone you love them (only say it if it's true!)

- Be a good listener

- Compliment someone in front of others

- Hold the elevator for someone

- Leave some extra coins in the change section of a vending machine

- Give your umbrella to somebody in the rain

KINDNESSMATTERS

- Write down a list of things you love about your other half and place it in an envelope addressed to them

- Send dessert to another table when out dining in a restaurant

- Purchase some extra dog or cat food and drop it off at an animal shelter

- Keep an extra umbrella at work and let someone borrow it on his or her way home if there's a sudden downpour

- Adopt an animal online (snow leopards seem popular)

- Make two lunches and give one away

- When going out with friends, offer to be the designated driver – it's healthier, and you'll save money

- Let somebody else have your parking space

- Buy sunscreen for someone on a sunny day

- Arrange to give blood

"At the end of each day, take a moment to sit in silence and reflect on all the moments of kindness you created."
- John Magee

KINDNESSMATTERS

Facebook Community

I feel empowered to start this section of the book by saying, "I love you" to the whole of our Kindness Community!

If you would have told me back in 2012 that I would have thousands of friends from all around the globe who check-in daily on social media to share their kindness stories, along with helping support me and my global kindness vision, I would have said, 'whatever have you been drinking you need to cut down on that stuff!' Being serious, though, the people I have met over the past five years through my vision have become true friends; some even better than those I have grown up with and known all my life.

I am still overwhelmed by how many amazing people there are out there in the world who are making a massive difference in other people's lives, raising awareness on just how much Kindness Matters.

I have had the privilege of being contacted by / meeting people from all over the globe during the building of our Kindness Community. I make an example of a fellow Kindness Ambassador and author of The Kindness Diaries, Leon Logothetis, who by sheer coincidence or synchronicity ended up in our global Kindness Community on Facebook when an existing member added him. What struck me about Leon is how he gave up everything and got out of the 'rat race' to travel the world and share his kindness along the way by relying on random acts of kindness to get him to where he is today. I think if you were to ask him how he did this, he would tell you that he followed his heart. I highly recommend you visit his website at www.leonlogothetis.com if you can.

We cannot underestimate the power of having a global community of Kindness Ambassadors who are all like-minded people and who all wake up each morning with a common goal to spread more kindness and touch the hearts and minds of people on a D.A.I.L.Y basis. What I love about our Kindness Community is how they inspire me and help me understand that there is a world of people out there who believe in kindness and the power it can have to change the world.

When you read the stories in this section from people who contribute from different geographical locations around the globe, you will notice a common theme whereby ALL of the individuals are motivated by wanting to be the kindness they wish to see in the world. They all share a desire to be of service to others.

It is with a grateful heart that I am empowered by these people in our Kindness Community and know that you will be too. You will be motivated by the stories you are about to read. You may even be inspired to join our Kindness Community yourself - if you haven't done so already. Either way, I hope you will reach out.

On Day 1 of my Kindness Matters 30 Day challenge, I was out doing some shopping in Preston at the local retail park and helped an elderly woman to get down the stairs at a camping store. I then made sure I ran back up the stairs to inform her husband where she had gone. God love the poor old chap - he was looking inside tents for her!

Scott Parsons

I bought two pasties for a quid in our local bakery yesterday and gave one to a homeless guy I'd seen on my way down there. I think I'm going to make it a habit of being kind and doing random acts of kindness, as it's not like it's an expensive thing to do.

Martin Ainsworth

It was a lovely afternoon and my son and I were playing in the garden and enjoying the new pet chickens that we had recently purchased. They had been happily laying eggs when my son noticed that we had a new neighbour moving in next door. I thought to myself that I could do a random act of kindness so I popped around to the new neighbour's house with half a dozen fresh eggs from the chickens. I walked away thinking what a (smashing) random act of kindness that was!

Kelly Fletcher

I got a flat tyre this morning when driving, and while I was waiting for the breakdown company, a gentleman came out of

his house to ask me if help was coming and would I like a brew while I waited. On the way back home that night I posted him a thank you note and a lucky dip for the coming Lotto draw.
Paul Hollie

The greatest good you can do for another is not just to share your riches, but also to reveal to him his own.

I took it upon myself to pack up lots of toys, clothes and gadgets that my son no longer wants or needs. Some items had never even been played with, worn or used! I simply took them to a local charity shop, as I knew other little boys would love them.
Claudia Thomson

My random act of kindness involved assisting an elderly woman whilst I was in a shop in town. I had heard this eighty-something lady shout over to me in a strong regional accent. She couldn't reach an item at the back of the fridge. Not only was it at the back, it was on the bottom shelf. Leaving all my glamour aside, I got down on all fours to retrieve the item for her basket. I felt like a true hero!
Lisa Welsh

I came out of my local shop not long ago and there was a lady struggling to get out of her car. She was disabled and when I approached her she told me she was trying to post her brother's birthday card in a box down the street. It was throwing it down with rain and I got soaked, but I told her to stay in the car while I posted the card for her.

Owen Mcgill

Whenever I purchase a meal deal in town, I always ask for a coffee as my drink option and then take it to somebody who looks like they need it more than me, whether they be busking or begging. It's only a simple act but always well received, especially when the weather is dreary.

Carmen Rickhard

The more sympathy you give, the less you need.

This morning I have messaged two friends who are both struggling with things in life at the moment, just to let them know I am thinking of them both and that my shoulders are here to cry on and my arms are open for hugs.

Paulette Merrin

Random act of kindness completed for today - I saw my neighbour earlier, an elderly man on his own. He had taken some parcels in for us while we were out. He told me in passing that he had sprained his ankle. He wouldn't take me up on any offers of help, so tonight I made a big batch of beef ragu and took a portion of it round to my neighbour's house so he could have something tasty for his tea.

Becky Hellier

Yesterday I called round to see one of my closest best friends who is not well. I made sure she was ok and ran her a bath!
Ali Lees

Kind words can be short and easy to speak, but their echoes are truly endless.

Yesterday I gave a lady the coffee that I had just bought. She looked like she needed it more than me!
Alison Fiona Williams

I practice this on a daily basis if the opportunity arises. In the supermarket, I often help people who look in need of help, perhaps if they're reaching for something. I help people find items they are looking for. I move abandoned trollies that would otherwise have made someone have to stop and get out of their car to move them before parking.

In other places, I'll always offer my seat on a bus or in the park. On other occasions, I have paid for people's shopping, carried their bags, helped people crossing the road, and reunited wandering dogs with their owners. I get a lot of pleasure from offering to help people, and when these people express gratitude in return, that's even better!
Nina Eveleigh

KINDNESSMATTERS

***Do one act of kindness each day of the year and
change 365 lives.***

Tell people about your random acts of kindness – it's the best
way to teach our children how to be kind, and to inspire others
to be kind, also.

Shameena Reidy

It's brilliant to check out free sites on the internet, as there are
often people on them asking for help. Today I picked up some
clothes for somebody who couldn't get there to pick them up
herself. I'd never even met her!

Emma Hammond

I asked the cashier in my local supermarket today to put another
person's shopping on my bill. The man in question (behind me
in the queue) initially declined but I told him about Random
Acts of Kindness and he accepted. He gave me the biggest
kiss on my cheek with a wonderful smile and a from the heart
"thank you". I felt a surge of happiness and inner peace.

Zynab Bah

Today's random act of kindness - I took my friend a cake into
work as I was passing by her office. She was chuffed to bits.

Katie Parker

KINDNESSMATTERS

I've been handing out £1 coins, one every day, to random people for the past year. Loads of people dubiously rejected my offer of a no-strings £1 coin being handed to them at first (we're a cynical bunch), so I ended up putting a lot of them on the floor.

Lessons learned:
1. There might not always be a catch with free money.
2. Look out for shiny objects on the ground.
Nathania Hartley

Remember there is no such thing as a small act of kindness. Every act creates a ripple of no logical end.

It's such a good feeling having a clear out at home. Today I put together 10 black bags of clothes, shoes and household stuff. My house is clear, and all of those bags have now gone to my local hospice. The items will either be used, or will be sold to raise money!
Sharon Armstrong

Do an act of kindness for someone else. Not because you should, but because you can.

Ok, so today I was shopping in the supermarket and the lady in front of me was packing up her shopping as the checkout operator finished putting her groceries through. The total came up and the lady declared she was £3 short. She asked the cashier if she could put some items back to reduce the total. I watched as the cashier selected some fresh meat from the bags. I chipped in at this point and paid the £3 – meat saved and back in the shopping bags. The lady just walked away! I was a little annoyed at first, but at least I did a nice thing!

Pam Clarkson

There are four young adults who work together and come into our cafe bar every morning. They're always smiling and so pleasant. I've even mentioned to their boss how polite they are. Today they came in as usual to order breakfast, and I gave them their drinks for free. I even bought their boss a drink later when he came in. They all asked why, and I said it's a Random Act of Kindness, and told them how they're just a lovely bunch of people who make me smile. So simple.

Emma Tapper

> *Wherever there is a human in need, there is an opportunity for kindness and to make a difference.*

I took it upon myself to complete an online survey for a lady who provided good service in a shop recently. She really appreciated the feedback as it was a competition for her at work. She deserves it so I hope she wins.

Samantha Pierce

I bought a man a pack of mints on Friday as he didn't have

enough money in the shop, and yesterday I gave a man in the launderette some of my powder and softener as the dispenser wasn't working. Feeling good!

Lynda Carter

This was a Random Act of Kindness from my amazing son, Cody, left on my bed for when I returned after a game of touch rugby. He had left me a strawberry lace to eat, and had made a bracelet from another. Very lucky mummy – especially as he loves strawberry laces!

Deena Pralat

> *Love and kindness are never wasted. They always make a difference. They bless the one who receives them, and they bless the one who gives them.*

Just been out for a meal with my family. I went to settle the bill with my mum. Just before we left, my six year old daughter pulled out of her pocket the 50p she got from the tooth fairy the previous evening and gave it to the waitress who had been serving us. She said, "That's for you". How kind!

Sharn Edwards

One night whilst out getting some bits from the local shop, I bought a EuroMillions ticket and posted it through the door of a random house on my walk back home!

Paul Hollie

Research has shown time and again that people who give to others, in small and large ways, tend to be happier and live longer. I want to live a long and happy life. How about you?

First of all, can I just say that it's very tricky do a Random Act of Kindness when in a rush on the London Underground! It's chaos, but I still found the opportunity on my last visit to help somebody up a flight of cramped stairs with a huge bag. There's always an opportunity out there.
Bob Eastwood

Before we left for the airport on the last day of our holiday, my son gave away lots of the things we had bought whilst we were there. So, he looked for other children and gave them pool toys, balls and inflatables.

Also on that holiday, I went diving into the sea after somebody had lost their wedding ring in there! I didn't find it, of course, but I had to try!

On the flight home, I thought about these things and decided to write an inspirational quote on a piece of paper and hide it in the seat pocket for a future passenger to read and hopefully feel good. I'm going to keep doing this one - leaving random notes where strangers may find them. My son thought it was a great idea so he is going to do it, too. Have a great day everyone.
Adam Green

Kindness is essential to mental peace.

A couple of weeks ago, I picked up a homeless man who was taking shelter in a doorway. He was a pensioner and was not well at all. I took him to McDonald's for a hot drink and then found him a place to stay for the night via a local charity. I couldn't leave the man in his state in the rain, and it made me feel better to just do something.

Amy Ainsworth

I spent some time today speaking with a young man with learning difficulties. I listened to him describing his collection of scarves. He was so enthusiastic.

Coincidentally, I bumped into him again six hours later and listened to his story all over again! It was the kindest thing to do.

Olwen Cross

Sometimes, it's really nice to just give someone a lift somewhere. I did that for an old friend today after I saw her at the bus stop. Plus, it was nice to have the company and the chat!

Lorraine Scholes

Real generosity is doing something nice for someone who will never find out.

KINDNESSMATTERS

Today I let a lady in Marks & Spencer go in front on me in the queue, even though she had tonnes more items than me. My reason? Her basket looked a lot heavier than mine!

Alison William

Random Acts of Kindness are an everyday occurrence in my life.

This week:

1. Collecting furniture/household stuff for a person in my community who had to start his life over with nothing.
2. Ringing a friend to ask how she was, knowing she was going through a tough time.
3. Giving a person a lift so that they could be with a loved one in need.
4. Accepting a shift at a job I'm not fond of because I knew that my colleague could really do with the break.

Gemma Wordsworth

The smallest act of kindness is worth more than the grandest intention.

So proud of my girl tonight! She was given £2 as a treat to spend in the shop, but absolutely blew me away with her first random act of kindness - donating £2 worth of tins to the food bank!

Jo Rigby

One act of kindness won't change the whole world, but it may change one person's world.

Tonight I rendered a checkout lady in the supermarket speechless when I bought her some fruit to break her fast while she worked. I then told her all about Random Acts of Kindness, and I hope she pays the kindness forward.
Jo Rigby

Be happy and do the best you can. Be good and kind.

I've told my friend Penny about Random Acts of Kindness. Penny does so much to help those around her, from gardening, decorating, dog sitting, sourcing useful tools, gadgets and gizmos, and often using money from her own pocket to help people out. She personalises her birthday cards with memorable photos... the list goes on! I often find that Penny has left me a bunch of fresh cut flowers on my doorstep. Lovely. More people should be like Penny.
Miz Terrell Tang

Driving through my local village to drop off my daughter, Evie, at her grandad's, I spotted the father of one of Evie's school friends. He was walking along the road with a petrol can – obviously his car must have broken down. It's a desolate country road, so he was in for a bit of a hike to find a petrol station!

Even though I knew I'd be late for work, I turned the car around and offered him a lift to the petrol station and back.
Derren Lee Poole

I supported my husband over the weekend with an annual local music festival raising money for local charities. We set it up five years ago in memory of our son's guitar teacher who died of cancer. It has grown from a one-day festival into a three-day spectacular due to its success. Over 20 bands play for free and the volunteers work all weekend giving up their time so that everyone has an amazing time bringing the community together for our local hospice! People can always give their time.
Sarah Fletcher

I always let people in/out in front of me in the car when I'm driving anywhere, even if I'm in a rush. Usually they don't really say/gesture 'thank you' or anything, but I don't take offence. Yesterday we were stuck in traffic and a guy was trying to get onto then main road, but I could see that all the cars in front of me wouldn't let him in even though they weren't getting anywhere fast, so I let him in and he waved 'thank you'.

Straight after that, he let someone out too, and it made me smile because I felt like even though it was a small Random Act of Kindness it was passed on straight away.
Shodease Allen-Dexter

FACEBOOK COMMUNITY

Kindness is the new you.

I ended up missing my train at 3 o'clock today so I decided to go and get a bit of food somewhere. As I was in the queue, I decided to do something I've wanted to do for ages... get a 'family feast' from the menu. I then took my order and walked off to find someone to share it with. His name was Billy. He was 50 years old and had been out on the street for over a year. He used to work in demolition. He supports Manchester United, and when he had a job he used to go regularly to the matches. I found out that Billy's family had fallen apart. All this info through taking the time to chat.

When I turned up with the food, Billy thought I was having a laugh. I really enjoyed sitting on the floor and eating with him. Again, how important it is to talk to each other as well.
John Richie

I helped my mate move his mum's furniture and belongings from her old house. It involved me driving down South to unload the furniture and drive back up North. By the end I'd helped them out by completing almost a 400 mile round trip.
Paul Hollie

I bought a bag of sweets in with my shopping today, and gave the sweets to the cashier after she had put them through the till.
Kris Domokos

Your greatness is measured by your kindness; your education and intellect by your modesty; your ignorance is betrayed by your suspicions and prejudices, and your real strength is measured by the consideration and tolerance you have for others.

I have to share the Random Act of Kindness I have just heard that Sofia, my six year old daughter, did on Tuesday. Her class was on a coach on the way back from a school trip, when the boy next to Sofia dropped and lost his 10p. He was quite upset so Sofia gave him 10p of her own money to make him feel better. The teacher found the 10p later on under the seat and the boy's mum told me what had happened and gave me 10p to give back to Sofia today. When I asked Sofia about it she said, "He looked really upset, and even though I really wanted my 10p, I gave it to him to make him feel better". Definite proud mummy moment.

Saira Rashid

Today I went to eat at a restaurant for lunch and I saw this elderly lady approaching the same restaurant, so I waited to hold the door for her. She was very thankful. She then told the waitress, "table for one", so I waited and hesitated but then I walked over and said, "I'm eating by myself too - would you like to have lunch together?"

KINDNESSMATTERS

She was ecstatic! We ate and we chatted, and I found out that she had spent the last decade living with her mum who had then recently passed away. I also found out that her aunt had recently gone into a nursing home, and so this lady (Delores) was having a bit of a tough time of things. We had a lovely time and I seemed to cheer her up. I'm so glad I got to meet, chat and eat with Delores – she gave me as much company as I gave her.

Learn to love without condition.

Talk without bad intention.

Give without any reason.

Today, myself and the kids were sitting on a bench in town enjoying an ice cream. After a few minutes, I noticed a man sitting in a doorway. I sat watching him for a little while noticing how people were just walking past and completely ignoring him.

I felt this was no way to treat a fellow human being, so when the kids had finished we went over for a chat. By this time, he had been joined by another man, who turned out to be his brother. They were both homeless and sleeping rough. We talked for a while and they told me a little about themselves. Then I got them both a warm drink. They were both very grateful and one of them gave my youngest child a Spiderman toy that he had found. It really touched me that somebody with so little could still find something to give.

Rosina Clarke

At the right time, a kind word from a stranger, or encouragement from a friend, can make all the difference in the world. Kindness is free, and most of it is priceless.

I was on a short trip away for the weekend at a hotel in the Lake District.

Whilst taking a seat at the hotel bar, I found a wallet under the chair. I was shocked that it contained several hundred pounds in cash. I was the only person in the bar and it would have been very easy to put the wallet in my pocket and leave the hotel. However, I handed the wallet to the person behind the bar and I felt quite content that I had made the right decision.

An hour or so later, a man rushed quickly into the bar and it was quite obvious to me that this was a person who had lost something. It turned out that I was correct and it was the man whose wallet I had found. He went straight to the bar to ask if anyone had handed in the wallet and looked exceptionally relieved when the lady who was working handed it back to him. When the lady pointed me out, the man came across to the group I was sat with and was so extremely happy that he had

got all his money, cards and photos back, he offered to buy the whole group a round of drinks as a way of showing his gratitude.
Trevor Tomes

I frame prints for a living. When several local people on my holiday helped me out when my car broke down recently, I treated them all to having prints framed. The farmer who made me a cup of tea as I waited got himself a picture of his favourite sheep!
Pat Tack

There is no better feeling in the whole wide world than to know that you have helped another human being who was in need.

I gave birth to my daughter six weeks ago and I'm so lucky to have the most amazing family and friends for support. They bought us lots of baby things which we are so grateful for.

Around the same time as my daughter's birth, a friend of mine left her partner due to domestic violence. There was a centre that she went to in our town which really supported her, along with lots of other women and children who had suffered through domestic violence.

I called the centre the other day and asked if it was ok to donate some things for the women in their refuge. I made up two big bags, with each containing a range of baby essentials, clothes, toiletries, nappies, wipes and coats, plus a blanket etc. Fantastic as these gifts were when given to me, I simply had too many and it seemed wrong that there were women and babies out there in my town who had nothing.

Having a new baby is meant to be a happy time. Hopefully, my gift bags will help bring some joy to those new and young mums who have otherwise suffered so much.

Danni Taylor

Kindness the most valuable gift you will give someone.

Yesterday I was enjoying a lovely evening out with friends. When we were leaving the place we had eaten, the waiters gave us some seeded buns for free to take home, as they had said they would only be throwing them out anyway. Whilst walking back to the car, there was a homeless gent sat beside the road. The three ladies with me all thought the same thing – let's give our food to this gent. He was very grateful for the food and the chat – which is always just as important.

I just wish businesses would stop throwing out good food and give it to people who really need it.

Margaret Shuttleworth

I am an animal lover and help run a local dog rescue charity. I also have a business I have recently set up from scratch, where I supply raw pet food. Whenever I see a homeless person with a pet, I always make sure to donate some food or water or a treat. Animals are important, too.

Kieron Mayers

You cannot get through a single day without having an impact on the world around you.

The other day I was driving behind a learner driver. She was doing 20mph on a 50mph road. I had watched a number of cars overtake her in frustration, all the while gesturing some not very nice things, but I decided to stay behind her because everybody has to learn. I didn't want to put her off and make her feel under pressure so I stayed a safe distance behind her and smiled. I made sure she could see my smile and her instructor held his hand up to say thank you. This is one of my first ever Random Acts of Kindness.

Hannah Kinloch

Kind people are my kinda people.

My son and I decided we were going to buy some chocolates in a shop, and then give them to someone randomly when the time felt right. A little later, we saw a lady on a bench looking a

little lost in thought. My son approached her and gave her the chocolates. I don't know who was happier – her or me!
Lady-Chantellé Baldwin

One thing you will never regret is being kind.

I was at Birmingham train station and my train was delayed so I went out for some fresh air. Whilst I was outside, I noticed a man looking deeply distressed and so I asked if he was OK. The reply was that he was a few quid short for his train ticket, so I gave him £5 and the look on his face was priceless. I wished him a Merry Christmas and went to board my train feeling very happy indeed!

It was Christmas, by the way!
Kimberley Falconer Allen

I held a Christmas party today for 40 elderly and lonely pensioners. We provided food, drinks, cards and a gift for them all. There were so many happy faces of people who would have otherwise been alone at Christmas; a time when nobody should be alone.
Julie Higgins

If it doesn't challenge you, it won't change you.

30 Day Challenge

Thank you, John, for writing such an inspirational book. I plan on recommending your 30 Day Challenge to friends, family and work colleagues, because I personally believe it will have a positive impact on them like it has done on me.

Tracy Johnson

From my 30 Day Challenge I gained a stronger sense of love and care for my fellow sisters and brothers. I gained a clear and concise understanding of the true values of kindness and giving back to a society that has forgotten what it means to just be kind.

Anthony West - Chicago

From day one of starting my 30 Day Challenge, I started to apply the concept with all the many people I came into contact with on a daily basis. I really reaped the benefits - as I hope they did, too!

Viv Bickham

The feeling of being kind to others and seeing their faces light up with a smile is the most wonderful feeling! This then encourages you to continue delivering acts of kindness on a daily basis, incorporating them into everything you do until it becomes habit and is easy to do. Not only is it easy, but it's free and can change someone's moment, someone's day and even someone's life. It makes you feel fantastic!

Amber Jane Davis - Sydney Australia

THE 30 DAY CHALLENGE

Good morning, afternoon, evening or possibly even good night wherever you are in the world.

As I write this section of the book, it is just after 4:30 in the morning, and I am up and awake doing my 'Miracle Morning' rituals. This morning feels different to most mornings, and I feel incredibly excited even at this ridiculous hour!

Do you remember when you were a child, and the excitement you would have the night before your birthday? I bet you can recall the sensation of all your excited thoughts and feelings.

Was your imagination running wild thinking of all the positive stuff that would be happening the next day; perhaps the anticipation of the gifts you may be receiving? Well, that is just how I am feeling right now. As I write this section of the book, I am overwhelmed with feelings of excitement and I am eternally grateful and feel honoured to be sharing this information with you; my friends and fellow Kindness Practitioners.

If you are anything like me or my kids you will love receiving gifts, whether it be for Christmas, Eid or on your birthday. The best ones are always the surprise gifts; the random gifts that you are not expecting and come to you out of the blue. Any random gift I receive that I was not expecting always puts me on a 'ten' on The Moody Meter.

I can relate kindness to giving and receiving gifts, because this is the whole vision behind what we are looking to achieve on a D.A.I.L.Y basis. We are committing on a D.A.I.L.Y programme to look for opportunities to live with an attitude of "I live to give". With our kindness, I honestly believe one of the greatest gifts we can ever give or receive is kindness.

By applying D.A.I.L.Y kindness, we are consistently gifting to and from people with our kindness.

I mean, come on - how beautiful is that?

We harness this power within ourselves that we can give our kindness freely. With all the kindness hints and tips within the book that you are holding in your hands right now, you have access to a fantastic amount of kindness that you can apply each day.

Now, anybody that knows me will know that I love acronyms. Let's take RAOK, for example - Random Acts of Kindness. So, I had to come up with an acronym that would best fit our vision for our global community. That acronym is D.A.I.L.Y, and you've read it a few times in this section already. So, what does it stand for?

THE 30 DAY CHALLENGE

Decision
Action
Inspiration
Learning
Yes

These are all of the positive words to remember on each day of your 30 Day challenge. Keep them in mind as you practice D.A.I.L.Y kindness.

Let me finish this section by asking you if you are you ready to have more joy, happiness and fulfilment in your life? I guess the answer to that is a big YES! Who wouldn't want more of those things in their life? Sharing kindness with others is a win-win situation, because let's not forget that "what you do comes back to you".

Turn over to the next page to begin your D.A.I.L.Y kindness journey, safe in the knowledge that you are going to have more joy, happiness and fulfilment in your life to make sure that you can come and join me at a 'ten' on The Moody Meter.

THE 30 DAY CHALLENGE

"It is in your moments of decision that your destiny is shaped."
- Anthony Robbins

Here we go, hold tight and enjoy the ride, because you are now about to embark upon the journey of your life, and what I am going to share with you now will not only ramp up your kindness, but It will also improve other areas of your life and the lives of others along the way. The first of our practice in our D.A.I.L.Y kindness is the power of decision making.

Let me ask you a question! If I could share with you some information that will transform your life for the better in every area of your life, would that be useful to you?

Come on, the answer to that question is a no-brainer.

For me, I am overwhelmed by the miraculous benevolent power of how when I make a decision to share my daily kindness with others, how I witness and watch my kind acts unfold in front of me and the positive impact it has on me and the person in receipt of my kind deed.

Just imagine the world full of like-minded individuals like you and I, waking each day and taking action to apply D.A.I.L.Y kindness to their life and the lives of others! Well, now you can, because you and I are kindred spirits, and because you

KINDNESSMATTERS

are reading this book we both have common ground. We are sharing the same daily journey and moving one step closer to achieving our (sustainable) GLOBAL vision, which is to create more Kindness Ambassadors and to spread more love and kindness into the world.

Let me share a story with you about a man from India who grew to inspire and motivate the lives of millions. You may have heard of this gentleman, he was called Mohandas Karamchand Gandhi. Gandhi had more than enough quality values, like his belief for non-violence and civil rights. Gandhi famously led Indians in challenging the British-imposed salt tax with the 400 km (250 mi) Dandi Salt March in 1930, and later called for the British to quit India in 1942.

He was imprisoned for many years, upon many occasions, in both South Africa and India. Gandhi attempted to practise non-violence and truth in all situations and advocated that others do the same. He lived modestly in a self-sufficient residential community and wore the traditional Indian dhoti and shawl, woven with yarn hand-spun on a charkha. He ate simple vegetarian food, and also undertook long fasts as a means of both self-purification and social protest.

In my neighbouring town of Darwen, Gandhi made a visit to India Mill, which was a great cotton factory, to challenge the management of the factory on the concept that Indian people, who were working for cheap labour, should be treated fairly. Gandhi understood the importance of equality, civil rights and non-violence to express a view in a non-confrontational manner.

He had a gift to help people understand that if they were not happy with something, how they could take responsibility and change it by becoming the change; famously coining the phrase "be the change you want to see in the world."

Personally, I believe the best way to promote non-violence is with kindness and compassion and by becoming the kindness we want to see in the world. Ok, I hear you say, so how can we spread more kindness in the world and become the kindness we want to see in the world? Well, thanks for asking! Whether you choose to do the 30 Day challenge or just dip in and out of your copy of this book, what I would encourage you to do is read your Kindness Matters Pledge on page 120 and then decide what act or acts of kindness you are going to apply the next day.

Once you have committed and decided what your act or acts of kindness are going to be, remember to go easy on yourself. We all have busy lifestyles, work, kids, friends, hobbies, and lots of different commitments. If you forget to apply one of your kind act or acts or the opportunity did not arise from what you had decided to apply, the key word here is to be FLEXIBLE and to ask yourself what you've learnt from this. There is something really compelling about decision-making and taking accountability and action....

"It's unrealistic to think that the future of humanity can be achieved only on the basis of prayer; what we need to do is take action." - Dalai Lama

Action

Not that I am a famous actor (YET), but I do like to bring out my thespian side when I am delivering my workshops or when I am delivering my keynote speeches. We now even have a Kindness Matters YouTube channel, and I know exactly what to do when the crew shout "Lights, Camera, Action!"

I actually have a pseudonym, whereby I go by the name of Mister Consequence, and when I deliver my thought-provoking keynote speeches they have a very powerful message about the importance of taking ACTION and how every action has consequences. When I deliver my talks, I encourage the audience not only to take action but to take MASSIVE action, because when we take massive action we get massive results. Think about it for a moment; everything you have in your life, your car, your home, your partner, kids etc, is because you made a decision. The actions you took from those decisions then became your reality.

I am convinced that we are responsible for our own happiness, and that when we take action with our kindness, it is a win-win situation. In giving, we indeed do receive, but we have to take action and commit to applying our kind deeds daily.

What does the name Dan Wieden mean to you? Well, he is the founder of the Wieden+Kennedy Advertising Agency, and in 1998, the advertising phrase 'Just Do It' was coined in their offices. You will probably recognise this as the world famous branding for sports company, Nike. And didn't Dan and his team hit a winner by encouraging people to get into exercise by JUST DOING IT! What I am saying is, we have to TAKE ACTION and JUST DO IT - Just Do Kindness.

In 1990, my Mum and I had been homeless for over 2 years. Let me tell you it was a very challenging time for us, and when I look back now and reflect on what has got me to this point in my life some 20 years later, including writing this book and creating this Random acts of kindness movement, I see that although there were a lot of people around me who influenced me in one way or another, ultimately it was down to ME to take action. I began to understand that I was responsible for my happiness in my life, and that the only person who could change anything was me.

When we make a conscious decision with what kindness we are going to apply in our daily lives, we become the kindness

KINDNESSMATTERS

we want to see in the world. Additionally, we come to inspire others...

"Your mind is a powerful thing. When you fill it with positive thoughts, your life will start to change." - Kushandwizdom

Inspiration

If I said to you that you are an inspiration to many people, including me, what would you say?

Or what if I said to you that most of your inspiration is done at a subconscious level, whereby you won't tend to notice when you are inspiring others?

The same is when we perform kind acts. We tend to forget that when we consciously make a decision to do our Random Acts of Kindness, how many people we influence and inspire with our kindness.

I recently read a book called "Ignite Inspiration" by an author named Lucy Hoger. In her book, Lucy talks a lot about inspiration and motivation, and how the primary driver is taking action.

Each day when we make a conscious decision to create random acts of kindness, or when opportunities arise where we can perform an act of kindness, there are always people watching - and remember, Monkey See, Monkey Do. The more we carry out our kind acts each day, the more people we inspire.

This leads me to a story. About a year ago, I was in town doing some shopping, and I noticed a young teenage boy drop a piece of litter. I made my way to the piece of litter, noticing a couple of people watching me. I then stalled, looked at the piece of litter, and bent down slowly, knowing there were people observing me and probably thinking why was I picking up that litter. I didn't so much want to clear up after anyone, but I wanted to counter the behaviour the teenage boy had shown. I view these acts as Undercover Kindness. I may not be able to change the boy's behaviour or anybody else's behaviour, but I can change or modify my own behaviour, and by doing so, I can inspire others to think about their conduct and their kindness.

Please understand that when you are applying your daily kindness and random acts of kindness, others, as well as yourself, are learning from the experience. All life is experiential learning...

"Learning is the beginning of wealth. Learning is the begining of health. Learning is the beginning of spirituality. Searching and learning is where the miracle process all begins."
- Jim Rohn

KINDNESSMATTERS

Learning

Some might say that "every day is a school day". My late father also had a saying where he would say to me, "the longer you live, the more you learn, Johnny boy".

When you take a moment and think about it, life is just one big learning experience!

Whether we notice consciously or subconsciously, every day we learn something new. I still find it fascinating that as human beings we have the capacity to acquire new skills and then apply them to our lives to improve how we function in the world.

When I work as a life coach I have a technique which I share with my participants in all my sessions, whereby I always give them a CTA - "call to action". Through this, we set a benchmark for that week and then evaluate it the following week. This is known as reflective practice. For example, I was once working with somebody who was struggling with self-confidence and low self esteem. I encouraged my client for that week to open up as many doors for people as possible (might sound a little bit tedious) but get this, because when my client came back the following week, they said that when they opened up doors most people were very polite and smiley and thankful, and this made them feel great. They said that through the interactions they felt respected.

What I am getting at here is that developing new skills daily and trying new things are all experiential learning.

I would like to share with you a technique I do myself every night before bed. One of my participants called it Time Travel. Consider this your Kindness Matters call to action:

When you go to bed at night, play your day back through your mind. Pause and stop on events you recall from the day and ask yourself the following questions:

- What have you learned from today?
- What did you contribute today?
- What did you enjoy today?

I learnt these techniques from a book by Tony Robbins called "Awakening The Giant Within", and these practices have helped me no end in spreading more loving kindness into the world. They have also brought a sense of well-being and so much peace into my life. I hope this Call to Action does the same for you.

Yes

"Hey...I'm saying 'Yes' to life...because you gotta say 'Yes' to life... I'm in a secret covenant...That sounded naughty."
- Jim Carrey from the movie Yes Man.

Have you seen the movie 'Yes Man'? Whether the answer is Yes (see what I did there) or No, let me share with you an overview of the film. Jim Carrey's character is a little fed up with his job and life in general, and is still on the mend from a broken relationship, when he coincidentally comes across an old friend who he has not seen for years. It transpires there has been a significant change in the guy, and he tells Jim's character that this is because he's been to see a guru who explained that the secret to living a life of happiness and freedom is by learning to say yes more often.

What I love about the concept of this movie is how learning to say yes more of the time empowers us. Now I am not saying for one minute that you have to say yes to absolutely everything, because that would be silly.

What I am saying from a kindness point of view, is that as we go about our daily lives, sometimes we are that busy running around that we miss lots of opportunities to say yes to being kind. Here is the thing - each day by taking the time to say yes when people ask us for some help instead of saying "no I am too busy" or I have to be someplace, we can really change the world.

Honestly, give it go, and catch yourself just before you say no to someone or something. Become aware and then say to yourself when you say Yes, you are being kind and of service to another human.

The Kindness Matters Pledge

Now that you have committed to your Kindness Matters 30 Day challenge, every night before bed, read the Kindness Matters Pledge, safe in the knowledge that when you wake the next morning, it is then that you will begin to share your kindness with others.

Step 1:

I have read a Kindness Matters story and the Kindness Matters hints and tips, and I have decided which act of kindness I am going to apply tomorrow, safe in the knowledge that my acts of kindness are going to have a positive impact on the person that receives them. I am also going to be open to all the kindness and Random Acts of Kindness possibilities that arise during my day, which have not been planned. When I have applied any kind act, I will say to myself:

I am grateful that all my kindness matters and makes a difference.

Step 2:

I let go of any limiting belief about my kind acts, not making a difference, or thinking that I am not a kind person. I will let go of any limiting beliefs that are holding me back from understanding just how much I matter to people. I accept that I am a part of everything and everything is a part of me, and

KINDNESSMATTERS

therefore when there is an opportunity for me to be kind and compassionate to another person, let me take that opportunity that has been gifted to me to use that opportunity for a force for good. I know that as I give to others, I give to myself.

Step 3:

Tomorrow at the end of my day I will dedicate this time (.............................) and I will record my kindness from my day in my Kindness Journal.

Step 4:

I will take the time to reflect on my day and travel back in time through my day with my imagination to pause and reflect on the events from my day. I will ask myself:

- What acts of kindness did I give today?
- What did I learn from my kindness today?
- What did I enjoy most about my kindness today?

The Kindness Matters Vow

I vow that with every breath, word, and step, I will be open to all the possibilities that arise in my day to be kind, and compassionate. Therefore, if there is an opportunity for me to be kind and apply a random act of kindness, let me grasp that opportunity and be of service, safe in the knowledge that all my kind acts make a difference. I vow from this day forward that no matter what challenges life throws at me, I will live with an attitude of "I live to give", knowing that all of my Kindness Matters.

Recording your Kindness

Recording our daily acts of kindness is an extremely powerful tool, as it helps us to reflect on our current and past actions. It can help us to recognise all the good we do in our daily lives.

Sometimes, we can get bogged down with the kids, work and the general 'daily grind'. However, finding a suitable time in the day that is right for us to record our kindness and random acts of kindness and to reflect on our kind acts can have huge health and psychological benefits. By writing about your kindness and random acts of kindness on a daily basis, you will begin to develop a greater awareness of how your kind and compassionate deeds have a significant impact on you and your wider community.

Life can be so unpredictable. Recording your random acts of kindness gives you time to reflect, and has been proven to help raise self-esteem, and, more importantly, can help you to gain resilience and give you tools for the future to apply in times of need.

KINDNESSMATTERS

How to journal your 30 Day challenge

1. The Kindness Matters 30 Day challenge is all about you and your experience. Whatever you write should be from your heart and form part of your own personal journey.

2. Trusting the process and committing to doing your bit each day will increase your feelings of well-being and sense of purpose.

3. Recording your Random Acts of Kindness at bed-time can help put you in a relaxing state ready for a good night's sleep.

4. When you are completing your 30 Day challenge, fully associate back into the experience and write what you could see, hear and feel from when you carried out your act of kindness.

5. As you complete your Kindness Matters 30 Day challenge, it's useful to stop and think of the effects your acts of kindness had on any other people who were involved.

6. Love and accept yourself. Understand that we are learning and growing, and that we are all doing our best with what we know in each moment of time. You have so much to give to the world and you can contribute to making it a better place. Recording your kindness experience will remind and help you understand just how much you matter.

KINDNESSMATTERS

People coming together as a community can make things happen.

My 30 Day Challenge

What acts of kindness have you shown today?

For others

_____

_____

For the environment

_____

_____

_____

For yourself

_____

_____

How would you rate yourself on your acts of kindness today? *Please tick one heart only

POOR	FAIR	GOOD	VERY GOOD	EXCELLENT
1 2	3 4	5 6	7 8	9 10

What act of kindness could you have shown today, but didn't?

_____

_____

_____

Today's question: *I believe in kindness because...*

_____

_____

_____

KINDNESSMATTERS

What acts of kindness have you shown today?

For others

_____

_____

_____

For the environment

_____

_____

_____

For yourself

_____

_____

How would you rate yourself on your acts of kindness today? *Please tick one heart only*

POOR		FAIR		GOOD		VERY GOOD		EXCELLENT	
1	2	3	4	5	6	7	8	9	10

What act of kindness could you have shown today, but didn't?

_____

_____

_____

Today's question: *I believe in kindness because...*

_____

_____

KINDNESSMATTERS

What acts of kindness have you shown today?

For others

For the environment

For yourself

How would you rate yourself on your acts of kindness today? *Please tick one heart only*

POOR	FAIR	GOOD	VERY GOOD	EXCELLENT
1 2	3 4	5 6	7 8	9 10

What act of kindness could you have shown today, but didn't?

Today's question: *I believe in kindness because...*

KINDNESSMATTERS

What acts of kindness have you shown today?

For others

For the environment

For yourself

How would you rate yourself on your acts of kindness today? *Please tick one heart only

POOR		FAIR		GOOD		VERY GOOD		EXCELLENT	
1	2	3	4	5	6	7	8	9	10

What act of kindness could you have shown today, but didn't?

Today's question: *I believe in kindness because...*

What acts of kindness have you shown today?

For others

For the environment

For yourself

How would you rate yourself on your acts of kindness today? *Please tick one heart only*

POOR	FAIR	GOOD	VERY GOOD	EXCELLENT
1 2	3 4	5 6	7 8	9 10

What act of kindness could you have shown today, but didn't?

Today's question: *I believe in kindness because...*

KINDNESSMATTERS

What acts of kindness have you shown today?

For others

_____

_____

_____

For the environment

_____

_____

_____

For yourself

_____

_____

How would you rate yourself on your acts of kindness today? *Please tick one heart only*

POOR		FAIR		GOOD		VERY GOOD		EXCELLENT	
1	2	3	4	5	6	7	8	9	10

What act of kindness could you have shown today, but didn't?

_____

_____

_____

Today's question: *I believe in kindness because...*

_____

_____

_____

What acts of kindness have you shown today?

For others

For the environment

For yourself

How would you rate yourself on your acts of kindness today? *Please tick one heart only

POOR	FAIR	GOOD	VERY GOOD	EXCELLENT
1 2	3 4	5 6	7 8	9 10

What act of kindness could you have shown today, but didn't?

Today's question: *I believe in kindness because...*

KINDNESSMATTERS

What acts of kindness have you shown today?

For others

_____

_____

_____

For the environment

_____

_____

_____

_____

For yourself

_____

_____

_____

How would you rate yourself on your acts of kindness today? *Please tick one heart only

POOR	FAIR	GOOD	VERY GOOD	EXCELLENT
1 2	3 4	5 6	7 8	9 10

What act of kindness could you have shown today, but didn't?

_____

_____

_____

Today's question: *I believe in kindness because...*

_____

_____

_____

What acts of kindness have you shown today?

For others

For the environment

For yourself

How would you rate yourself on your acts of kindness today? *Please tick one heart only*

POOR		FAIR		GOOD		VERY GOOD		EXCELLENT	
1	2	3	4	5	6	7	8	9	10

What act of kindness could you have shown today, but didn't?

Today's question: *I believe in kindness because...*

KINDNESSMATTERS

What acts of kindness have you shown today?

For others

For the environment

For yourself

How would you rate yourself on your acts of kindness today? *Please tick one heart only

POOR		FAIR		GOOD		VERY GOOD		EXCELLENT	
1	2	3	4	5	6	7	8	9	10

What act of kindness could you have shown today, but didn't?

Today's question: *I believe in kindness because...*

KINDNESSMATTERS

What acts of kindness have you shown today?

For others

For the environment

For yourself

How would you rate yourself on your acts of kindness today? *Please tick one heart only*

POOR	FAIR	GOOD	VERY GOOD	EXCELLENT
1 2	3 4	5 6	7 8	9 10

What act of kindness could you have shown today, but didn't?

Today's question: *I believe in kindness because...*

KINDNESSMATTERS

What acts of kindness have you shown today?

For others

For the environment

For yourself

How would you rate yourself on your acts of kindness today? *Please tick one heart only*

POOR		FAIR		GOOD		VERY GOOD		EXCELLENT	
1	2	3	4	5	6	7	8	9	10

What act of kindness could you have shown today, but didn't?

Today's question: *I believe in kindness because...*

What acts of kindness have you shown today?

For others

_____

_____

_____

For the environment

_____

_____

_____

_____

For yourself

_____

_____

_____

How would you rate yourself on your acts of kindness today? *Please tick one heart only*

POOR	FAIR	GOOD	VERY GOOD	EXCELLENT
1 2	3 4	5 6	7 8	9 10

What act of kindness could you have shown today, but didn't?

_____

_____

_____

Today's question: *I believe in kindness because...*

_____

_____

_____

KINDNESSMATTERS

What acts of kindness have you shown today?

For others

_____

_____

_____

For the environment

_____

_____

_____

For yourself

_____

_____

_____

How would you rate yourself on your acts of kindness today? *Please tick one heart only*

POOR		FAIR		GOOD		VERY GOOD		EXCELLENT	
1	2	3	4	5	6	7	8	9	10

What act of kindness could you have shown today, but didn't?

_____

_____

_____

Today's question: *I believe in kindness because...*

_____

_____

_____

KINDNESSMATTERS

What acts of kindness have you shown today?

For others

_____

_____

For the environment

_____

_____

_____

For yourself

_____

_____

How would you rate yourself on your acts of kindness today? *Please tick one heart only

POOR		FAIR		GOOD		VERY GOOD		EXCELLENT	
1	2	3	4	5	6	7	8	9	10

What act of kindness could you have shown today, but didn't?

_____

_____

_____

Today's question: *I believe in kindness because...*

_____

_____

KINDNESSMATTERS

What acts of kindness have you shown today?

For others

For the environment

For yourself

How would you rate yourself on your acts of kindness today? *Please tick one heart only*

POOR		FAIR		GOOD		VERY GOOD		EXCELLENT	
1	2	3	4	5	6	7	8	9	10

What act of kindness could you have shown today, but didn't?

Today's question: *I believe in kindness because...*

What acts of kindness have you shown today?

For others

_____

_____

For the environment

_____

_____

_____

For yourself

_____

_____

How would you rate yourself on your acts of kindness today? *Please tick one heart only*

POOR	FAIR	GOOD	VERY GOOD	EXCELLENT
1 2	3 4	5 6	7 8	9 10

What act of kindness could you have shown today, but didn't?

_____

_____

_____

Today's question: *I believe in kindness because...*

_____

_____

_____

KINDNESSMATTERS

What acts of kindness have you shown today?

For others

_____

_____

_____

For the environment

_____

_____

_____

_____

For yourself

_____

_____

How would you rate yourself on your acts of kindness today? *Please tick one heart only*

POOR		FAIR		GOOD		VERY GOOD		EXCELLENT	
1	2	3	4	5	6	7	8	9	10

What act of kindness could you have shown today, but didn't?

_____

_____

_____

Today's question: *I believe in kindness because...*

_____

_____

_____

What acts of kindness have you shown today?

For others

For the environment

For yourself

How would you rate yourself on your acts of kindness today? *Please tick one heart only*

POOR	FAIR	GOOD	VERY GOOD	EXCELLENT
1 2	3 4	5 6	7 8	9 10

What act of kindness could you have shown today, but didn't?

Today's question: *I believe in kindness because...*

KINDNESSMATTERS

What acts of kindness have you shown today?

For others

For the environment

For yourself

How would you rate yourself on your acts of kindness today? *Please tick one heart only*

POOR		FAIR		GOOD		VERY GOOD		EXCELLENT	
1	2	3	4	5	6	7	8	9	10

What act of kindness could you have shown today, but didn't?

Today's question: *I believe in kindness because...*

KINDNESSMATTERS

What acts of kindness have you shown today?

For others

For the environment

For yourself

How would you rate yourself on your acts of kindness today? *Please tick one heart only

POOR	FAIR	GOOD	VERY GOOD	EXCELLENT
1 2	3 4	5 6	7 8	9 10

What act of kindness could you have shown today, but didn't?

Today's question: *I believe in kindness because...*

KINDNESSMATTERS

What acts of kindness have you shown today?

For others

For the environment

For yourself

How would you rate yourself on your acts of kindness today? *Please tick one heart only*

POOR		FAIR		GOOD		VERY GOOD		EXCELLENT	
1	2	3	4	5	6	7	8	9	10

What act of kindness could you have shown today, but didn't?

Today's question: *I believe in kindness because...*

What acts of kindness have you shown today?

For others

For the environment

For yourself

How would you rate yourself on your acts of kindness today? *Please tick one heart only*

POOR	FAIR	GOOD	VERY GOOD	EXCELLENT
♡1 ♡2	♡3 ♡4	♡5 ♡6	♡7 ♡8	♡9 ♡10

What act of kindness could you have shown today, but didn't?

Today's question: *I believe in kindness because...*

KINDNESSMATTERS

What acts of kindness have you shown today?

For others

For the environment

For yourself

How would you rate yourself on your acts of kindness today? *Please tick one heart only*

POOR	FAIR	GOOD	VERY GOOD	EXCELLENT
1 2	3 4	5 6	7 8	9 10

What act of kindness could you have shown today, but didn't?

Today's question: *I believe in kindness because...*

What acts of kindness have you shown today?

For others

_____

_____

_____

For the environment

_____

_____

_____

_____

For yourself

_____

_____

_____

How would you rate yourself on your acts of kindness today? *Please tick one heart only*

POOR	FAIR	GOOD	VERY GOOD	EXCELLENT
1 2	3 4	5 6	7 8	9 10

What act of kindness could you have shown today, but didn't?

_____

_____

_____

_____

Today's question: *I believe in kindness because...*

_____

_____

_____

KINDNESSMATTERS

What acts of kindness have you shown today?

For others

For the environment

For yourself

How would you rate yourself on your acts of kindness today? *Please tick one heart only

POOR	FAIR	GOOD	VERY GOOD	EXCELLENT
1 2	3 4	5 6	7 8	9 10

What act of kindness could you have shown today, but didn't?

Today's question: *I believe in kindness because...*

KINDNESS MATTERS

What acts of kindness have you shown today?

For others

For the environment

For yourself

How would you rate yourself on your acts of kindness today? *Please tick one heart only*

POOR	FAIR	GOOD	VERY GOOD	EXCELLENT
1 2	3 4	5 6	7 8	9 10

What act of kindness could you have shown today, but didn't?

Today's question: *I believe in kindness because...*

KINDNESSMATTERS

What acts of kindness have you shown today?

For others

_____

_____

_____

For the environment

_____

_____

_____

_____

For yourself

_____

_____

_____

How would you rate yourself on your acts of kindness today? *Please tick one heart only*

POOR	FAIR	GOOD	VERY GOOD	EXCELLENT
1 2	3 4	5 6	7 8	9 10

What act of kindness could you have shown today, but didn't?

_____

_____

_____

_____

Today's question: *I believe in kindness because...*

_____

_____

_____

KINDNESSMATTERS

What acts of kindness have you shown today?

For others

_____

_____

_____

For the environment

_____

_____

_____

_____

For yourself

_____

_____

_____

How would you rate yourself on your acts of kindness today? *Please tick one heart only

POOR		FAIR		GOOD		VERY GOOD		EXCELLENT	
1	2	3	4	5	6	7	8	9	10

What act of kindness could you have shown today, but didn't?

_____

_____

_____

Today's question: *I believe in kindness because...*

_____

_____

_____

KINDNESSMATTERS

What acts of kindness have you shown today?

For others

For the environment

For yourself

How would you rate yourself on your acts of kindness today? *Please tick one heart only*

POOR		FAIR		GOOD		VERY GOOD		EXCELLENT	
1	2	3	4	5	6	7	8	9	10

What act of kindness could you have shown today, but didn't?

Today's question: *I believe in kindness because...*

KINDNESSMATTERS

155 |

"This is the beginning of a new day.
You have been given this day to use as you
will.
You can waste it or use it for good.
What you do today is important because you
are exchanging a day of your life for it.
When tomorrow comes, this day
will be gone forever;
in its place will be something that you
have left behind...
let it be something good."

- Japanese Proverb

KINDNESSMATTERS

Since I finished writing Kindness Matters there has been so much support predominately from my private community on Facebook. Visit www.kindnessmatters.co.uk and join in the community now to meet the rest of the family and thousands of like-minded fellow Kindness Ambassadors like you and I who wake each day to spread more kindness into the world.

Would I be off the mark to share with you my lifetime vision? It has always been my lifetime goal before I depart this planet, which for the record I hope is not until I am long in the tooth and my late 90's to have an annual month for Kindness Matters and more importantly a sustainable movement for the future generations which will be sharing kindness for families, communities, schools and individuals. Alright, I think you get where I am going with this- everybody having a go at the 30 Day Challenge.

Just imagine us having an official month of 30 Days of Kindness, let's say every September is the official month whereby communities, families, schools, businesses and individuals from all over the globe sign up to do the Kindness Matters 30 Day Challenge. I mean people could still do the 30 Day Challenge any month of the year, just the official month being September.

How powerful would that be? And how much kindness could

we share with the world? We are talking a Tsunami of Kindness rippling throughout the globe.

What do you think is stopping you and I in making this happen? I will tell you what is stopping us- NOTHING.

I believe collectively we can achieve this vision by 2020 and do you know why? Because the journey of a thousand miles has to begin with the first step and we have already taken that step.

WHAT I AM AIMING TO ACHIEVE FOR THE GLOBAL MOVEMENT

- To have a Celebrity Kindness Ambassador in each hometown/city.

- My hometown of Blackburn with Darwen to be recognised as a Kindness Community.

- Local authorities, schools, community groups, families and individuals to do the 30 Day Challenge.

- John Magee Global Kindness Matters tour.

- Speak on TED EX and share my global vision.

- My own kindness Matters TV series

KINDNESSMATTERS

2020 VISION

Recently, a big step towards my 2020 vision was complete. I had a meeting with a global celebrity who has agreed to become the first Kindness Ambassador for my hometown with a view for different stars to sign up, and become Kindness Ambassadors for their hometown/city -how good is that!

I will leave you a parting gift to whom the celebrity is... let's just say he is the four times world superbike champion ;-).

Let me finish by saying this. In life, there will always be people who think your vision/ideas are a bit far out and not achievable, but all that we are is our thoughts. Don't ever let anybody tell you that you can't achieve what you are THINKING.

Just take action, get up daily, keep moving forward to what you WANT, and more importantly what you believe in.

It is only a matter of time before your vision will become your reality.

I look forward to you joining me and my global community. Join the movement now visit www.kindnessmatters.co.uk .

"The ones who are crazy enough to think they can change the world, are the ones that do." - Steve Jobs

KINDNESSMATTERS

"**Kindness in words creates confidence.**
Kindness in thinking creates profoundness.
Kindness in giving creates love."

- Lao Tzu

BOOKS FOR THE JOURNEY

These books have inspired my journey, and without a doubt I believe that they have transformed my life. My wish is that they bring you happiness, well being and inner peace to accompany you along your kindness journey.

Simply type these titles into your search engine to source the best place to pick up a copy.

- The Miracle Morning - Hal Elrod
- Change Your Thoughts, Change Your Life - Dr Wayne Dyer
- The Art Of Happiness -The Dalai Lama and Howard C. Cutler
- The 7 Habits Of Highly Effective People - Dr Stephen R. Covey
- Awaken The Buddha Within - Lama Surya Das
- The Power Of Now - Eckhart Tolle
- Harmonic Wealth - James Arthur Ray
- The Secret - Rhonda Byrne
- Living Magically - Gill Edwards
- The Prophet - Kahlil Gibran
- The Science Of Getting Rich - Wallace D. Wattles
- Awaken The Giant Within - Tony Robbins
- I'm OK, You're OK - Thomas A. Harris
- A Course in Miracles - Foundation for Inner Peace

"I live to empower mankind because mankind empowers me."

- John Magee

BOOK JOHN TO SPEAK

Book John now to speak at your event! Please email hello@ kindnessmatters.co.uk

Speaking at your event, John is guaranteed to inspire, motivate and entertain your audience with his unique style of speaking. Your attendees will benefit from John's experience, and the messages he shares with them are sure to transform their outlook on life.

John's high energy and immensely positive approach to encourage his audience to take action and apply daily kindness will bring about an awareness of how you can have more happiness,well being, joy and inner peace in your life, whilst simultaneously ensuring the same outcomes in the lives of others.

"I have never witnessed an audience sit for an hour where you could literally hear a pin drop. The audience were truly spellbound by John's story of how much Kindness Matters."
Bob Eastwood - *Former Chief Superintendent, Lancashire Police*

"I have had the pleasure of speaking on stage with John Magee on BBC television during the 'A Way Out' project. He is by far one of the most powerful and thought provoking speakers that I have had the pleasure of working with. John is a true testament to how one person can overcome adversity and use the challenges that they have faced to inspire, motivate and raise aspirations for people so that they can succeed by adopting the universal language of kindness."

Richard McCann - *Professional Speaker & #1 International Bestselling Author of 'Just A Boy'*

"Our staff and students have worked with John Magee since 2012. I have been really impressed by the positive impact that his talks and workshops have had on all involved. He delivers his messages in a way that easily engages young people in particular. John empowers our students and staff and provides them with really helpful guidance and support at a level they understand and that can be applied across all aspects of our Academy. Everything that he does is student centred, pro-active and for the best interest of the Academy and community. I would strongly recommend John to speak at any school or college."

Chris Lickiss - *Head teacher, Unity Academy, Blackpool*

For more information or to book John at your next event email hello@kindnessmatters.co.uk

KINDNESSMATTERS

ACKNOWLEDGEMENTS

This book has been inspired through my own personal life experiences and through my awakening in 2008. I would also, however, like to make time to thank some other inspirational people…

My Mum, aka Nana Pat

Thank you for all you put up with in raising me. During the countless shenanigans with the law as a kid and my colourful past as an adult, you always stood by me and never gave up on me. I know where our Kathleen got all her kindness and affection for people from. Although we never had much at times, you helped me become the person I am today and you always believed in me putting something together to empower others. I know how excited you are to read this book, and I couldn't have done it without you. Thanks, Mum 381

My Dad, aka Ring Dinger (RIP)

Although it took us 30 years to get to the point of having an amazing relationship, I can't thank you enough for all your wisdom you used to share with me. It means even more now that you are not here. I would do anything to present this book to you and for you to see all I have become. I suppose I will have to continue to live by one of your favourite sayings and "paddle my own canoe". Miss you, Dad - every day. Thank you for everything; it all makes sense now.

Kathleen Magee (RIP)

I dedicated this book to you, my sister, because you were the kindest person I knew. I would do anything for you to be able to read this, and I would do anything to hear you say to me "I LOVE YOU". Nobody could ever spark me with those words like you did. I will continue to dedicate every talk to your memory, and will always picture you sitting in the audience looking up at me. I miss you, Kathleen. 381. Until we meet again.

My kids

The kindest gifts I have ever been given - Leona, Millie and Lucas. Thank you for listening to me most nights at the dinner table, out on walks or just in general. One day you will understand why I am so passionate. 381 Kids. Love, Daddy.

The Black Family

Lee, Sarah, Hollie, Evan and Grace. Lee, although you are my cousin you are like the brother I never had. I am truly thankful for all you have done and continue to do for me and my family. I can honestly say if it was not for your help back in 2008, I may not have ever written this book. You are an amazing person and I am truly fortunate to have you as my brother. Thanks again for all the Action Man figures and Sergio Tacchini clothing.

Jozef Magee, Shelli and the Kids

Thank you Jozef for always being there. All my life I have looked up to you and I am honoured to have you as part of my family. You have always been there for me and believed in me. A big thank you also to your Shelli (your backbone) for helping me through the tough times. Last but not least, thanks to your kids, Big Ben, Jozef (PC Magee), Liam (The Poacher), and Olivia for turning out to be such amazing children.

The Dunn Family

David, Hayley, Mia, Isaac, Lucia and Elijah. David, words cannot express the depths of my gratitude for what you have done for me. With all my projects you have always been there for me and believed in me. I have lost count of how many influential people you have introduced me to in your unofficial role as "Mr Blackburn". You are truly the greatest ambassador for our home town and I am honoured to call you my best mate.

Omar Clairvoyant Preston

Thank you for all you have done for me and all the messages you gave to me to keep me on the right path. All you said came true and still continues to help me to this day. Thank you for saving my life with what you revealed to me in the the early 1990s. It paved the way.

Scott and Victoria Moon

Since that very first time we met in your bar, Cafe de Realm, I knew we had something in common. You saw past my bravado and saw the real me. We clicked, and have had more ideas for making this world a better place than I can count. Don't ever let it stop. I would like to give love, adoration and respect to your son and my godson, Grayson Moon, RIP.

Tony Clarkson www.thesanctuaryofhealing.co.uk
Synchronicity. When we first met back in 2008, I would never have imagined the relationship we would have. Thank you for all you have done and continue to do in my life. You are a true friend and kindred spirit, and I am honoured to have you as a mentor.

Chris & Glenda Grimsley www.nlpinthenorthwest.co.uk
I am truly grateful that Tony Clarkson introduced me to you both. You have taught me everything I need to know about personal development and how to work with others. Your style of NLP training is out of this world, Chris. Thank you for being such a good mate and allowing me to model your style of training. I am honoured to stand on the shoulders of a giant like you. Thanks to my mate, The Burnley Buddha.

Eddie Mullany www.rootstoreality.co.uk
Since the day we met on our NLP course, I felt a connection with you. I cannot thank you enough for all your filming, producing and managing me as a person. You are a good friend and I am hugely excited for all the future work we are going to create globally to touch even more hearts and minds. Thanks mate.

KINDNESSMATTERS

ACKNOWLEDGEMENTS

Debra Sofia Magdalene www.mastery-path.com

You are an angel. Since we first met in 2009 and when you introduced me to Richard McCann, never would I have thought I'd be where I am now. Thank you for helping me understand what was going on and helping me understand that I was not going crazy! You are a very special lady and I am grateful for all that you give to empower mankind. I know you love your hugs so consider this a virtual hug until I see you next! Remember, 'Hugs not drugs, because drugs are for mugs'.

Jo Watson www.agoodwriteup.com (aka Ghosty)

Jo you are a star! How many years have we worked together now? And just how much have you had to put up with in dealing with my scatty approach to work?! All the secret meetings, having our midweek 2 for 1 curries with a laptop and a glass of Infadel... ;) Thank you for always letting me change this book, and much of my past works, at the 11th hour until we both know it's right. I look forward to us writing many more books and projects together, and bringing even more joy and opportunity to people's lives in the future. What a team we are! Thanks, Ghosty xxx

Rachel Allen (Rai)

You are a little darling. It is indeed a funny world. Just imagine if David never signed for Birmingham City Football club... would our paths still have crossed? I like to think they would have. You have been with me since 2012 and all you do and continue to do to keep our Facebook community buzzing with kindness energy is amazing. I look forward to us moving towards our Kindness Matters 2020 vision and all our great Google Hangout calls :)

Paul Bridge (Hoʻoponopono for Everyone), Naeem Akhtar (Peps)
You guys are amazing and I am honoured to have you in my life. Thank you for all the knowledge you have shared with me and the love and blessings I have recieved from my daily Hoʻoponopono practice. Thank You, Please Forgive Me, I'm Sorry, I Love You. POI.

Paul Jackson - Author Hoʻoponopono Secrets
Paul, your book Hoʻoponopono Secrets put a dint in the Universe and in my life. I have recommended your book to so many people. I cannot thank you enough for all the help with the publication of my own book, and all you have done for the Kindness Matters Movement. Thank You, Please Forgive Me, I'm Sorry, I Love You. POI.

Facebook Community - First up, eternal thanks to our Kindness Ambassadors Rae Allen, Claudia Thomson, Lorna McDonald, Tracy Johnson, Sarah Winfield, Chris Grayson, Paul Jackson, Paul Hubbard and Martin Ainsworth. You guys are instrumental within our community and I am grateful to have you all in my life.

ACKNOWLEDGEMENTS

Andy Neild & Clive Lawrence

Thanks for all you help over the years.

All of my Instagram friends at Foundr and the IGD Family

Nathan Chan @Foundr, Jesse Songe @Goalsmasher, David Hobson @davidmhobson, Jonathan Chan, Assya Barrette, Beck Ray @Happihabbits, Francesca Mch @francescamichaud, Farrukh Naeem Qadri @farrukhqadri @abudhabiimages, Kiman le Roux @flatlay_collective @linklay, Jorge Robert Sabbun Jr & all the IGCC family, Lucy Hoger @visionocity_magazine, Jackie Damelian @jackiemackdesigns @bigdreamshub, Luis Rivera @coachluisms, Arthur Luke @luke.online, Chris Ducker @chrisducker, Muoyo Okome @dailyspark, Birgit Smetana @inadventureland, Andy Willis @workingfromanywhere, Kristien Kettner @dronelookx, Zach Benson @thetravellerslist Volty Garcia @success_insider Tom Preikschat @cute.tv, Chris Duncan @Chrisduncanfitness
Thank you everybody for your kindness.

To Michael Kawula & David Boutin and all the crew at www. socialquant.net

I am eternally grateful for all you and your team have done to help me to build an amazing audience on Twitter. Social Quant are awesome and I will continue to spread the word. I look forward to you all coming to one of my USA workshops or events. Thank you for your kindness.

ACKNOWLEDGEMENTS

To my mentors, teachers, friends and work colleagues for their help: Adam Catterall, Linda Mason, Gavin Bell, Umbreen Ali, Vicky Cother, Ian Wiggins AKA Wiggy, Sheila Nelson for all my reflexology. Cheryl McGowan for all my Yoga. Lesley Manantan for all your creative work. Martha Friedlander, my Brazilian sister, you are such a beautiful soul... Harvey Mason for all your advice on social media and being a top mate. Steve Blackshaw for all the late nights helping me with the website. Mark Lamb for all your creative ideas and support. Roy Blake, Chris Lickiss and all the Unity staff for allowing me to inspire and motivate all your staff and Blackpool Community. Ashley Hackett, Dean Grice and Simon Smith for believing in me and helping spread my message. Steve Gray for all the continuous support and introducing me to the RATS. Bob Eastwood for everything you have done for me and continue to do for me and my family. Amanda Meachin (R Kid) I don't need to express how grateful I am to you because you already know! UTC. Imelda O'Keeffe for introducing me to the amazing world of NLP and all the endless books you shared with me. Last but certainly not least, my old boss Christine Lambe... thank you for coming to that meeting with me with Amanda back in 2008. Look where we are now. To all of the students and young people I have had the pleasure of working with – long may I continue to be of service to you.

Finally, to you, the reader: words cannot express how grateful I am that you have invested your time, energy and money into this book. I hope it brings you as much joy and happiness as it has brought me. Let's keep connecting on social media.

381 and thank you for your kindness.

Join the global movement www.kindnessmatters.co.uk along with thousands of others just like you who get so much out of life by performing daily acts of kindness and Random Acts of Kindness.

Become part of our global movement on social media:
www.thekindnesscoach.me
www.kindnessmatters.me

No matter what happens in life, be good to people. Being good to people is a wonderful legacy to leave.

ABOUT JOHN

John Magee is a certified Trainer & Master Practitioner in NLP (Neuro Linguistic Programming).

John is also a father, life coach, author, professional speaker, dedicated fundraiser and founder of www.thekindnesscoach. me – the website accompanying this book.

John has spent time during his busy career writing and designing a range of activity programmes for young people, families, communities and schools to help people reach their potential.
John lives by the mantra ...

"A greeting, gesture or a giggle.... Leave other people feeling better than before they met you." - John Magee

John has been interviewed by the BBC and appeared on local TV and national radio, as his ventures in speaking to over 100,000 young people, teachers, families and influential members of government work to spread his message.

"You are loved, cared for and thought about more than you ever possibly know." - John Magee

PAY IT FORWARD

This section of the book is about how you possess one of the greatest gifts there is – the gift of 'free will'.

Life is all about choices. When we consciously make positive choices in the present moment, they have positive consequences in the future.

Write your name here .... and pay your book forward as an act of kindness in itself.

If you have received this book as an act of kindness or a Random Act of Kindness, write your name below, then when you have used it, choose for yourself if you would like to pay the book forward and pass it on!

....
....
....
....
....

"My wish for you is that you continue. Continue to be who and how you are, to astonish a mean world with your kindness. Continue to allow humour to lighten the burden of your tender heart." - Maya Angelou

KINDNESSMATTERS

Join the community conversations and meet like minded people.

www.KindnessMatters.me

We'd love to hear from you!

Made in the USA
Las Vegas, NV
27 August 2021